Barbecue

A Pyramid Cooking Paperback

Barbecue

hamlyn

An Hachette UK Company
www.hachette.co.uk

A Pyramid Paperback

First published in Great Britain in 2005 by Hamlyn,
a division of Octopus Publishing Group Ltd,
2–4 Heron Quays, London E14 4JP
www.octopusbooksusa.com

This edition published in 2009

Copyright © Octopus Publishing Group Ltd
2005, 2009

Distributed in the U.S. and Canada by
Octopus Books USA:
c/o Hachette Book Group USA
237 Park Avenue
New York NY 10017

This material was previously published as
Barbecue

ISBN 978-0-600-62032-7

Printed and bound in China

10 9 8 7 6 5 4 3 2 1

Notes

Meat and poultry should be cooked thoroughly.
To test if poultry is cooked, pierce the flesh through
the thickest part with a skewer or fork—the juices
should run clear, never pink or red.

This book includes dishes made with nuts and nut
derivatives. It is advisable for those with known
allergic reactions to nuts and nut derivatives and
those who may be potentially vulnerable to these
allergies, such as pregnant and nursing mothers,
invalids, the elderly, babies, and children, to avoid
dishes made with nuts and nut oils. It is also
prudent to check the labels of preprepared
ingredients for the possible inclusion of nut
derivatives.

The Food and Drug Administration advises that
eggs should not be consumed raw. This book
contains some dishes made with raw or lightly
cooked eggs. It is prudent for more vulnerable
people, such as pregnant and nursing mothers,
invalids, the elderly, babies and young children,
to avoid uncooked or lightly cooked dishes made
with eggs.

Contents

The great outdoors

Nothing beats the laid-back fun of a summer barbecue—with skewers and steaks sizzling over the coals, big bowls of salad, chunks of crusty bread, and pitchers of ice-cold drinks. Whether you're enjoying a family get-together, entertaining friends, or planning an intimate dinner for two—a barbecue is always the perfect choice.

There's something about the word barbecue that screams "laid-back, leisurely food, and no-fuss fun." Everyone's always happy to lend a hand when it's needed, and to simply relax in the sun when it's not. Kids love being outside and will have a great time entertaining themselves (as long as they're well away from the cooking area). They'll also have a great appetite—so don't stint on the burgers and sausages. Barbecues are great when the sun goes down too and can be the perfect focus for laid-back entertaining on a balmy summer evening. There's nothing prettier than the flicker of garden candles or tea lights placed in empty jars around the garden while your guests mingle around the barbecue.

PLANNING FOR SUCCESS

There are really only three things you need for a successful barbecue: equipment, the right menu, and good weather. A little careful planning is all that's required, and even the most unpredictable element (the weather!) can be made to work.

1 First, you need to make sure you have the right equipment. This means a barbecue, fuel, ignition, tools for cooking, and water (in case of emergency).

2 Next, you need the right menu—with drinks, snacks to nibble, food for the barbecue, salads, accompaniments, and a dessert.

3 And, finally, you need to check the weather. If it's hot and sunny, make sure there's shade to sit in (as well as plenty of sunscreen and perhaps a few sunhats too!). If it looks as if it might rain, make sure there's comfortable shelter so that everyone can stay dry and still have fun.

CHOOSING THE RIGHT BARBECUE

There are almost as many barbecues to choose from as there are foods to cook on them, and which one to choose can be a mind-boggling affair. Built-in, portable, or disposable? Gas-, charcoal-, or wood-burning? Large or small? The easiest way to decide is to ask yourself what your own needs are:

• **How often will you use the barbecue?** If, realistically, you're going to have only a couple of barbecues every year, then there's no point in spending a lot of money on a top-of-the-range model. However, if you're going to barbecue every weekend, then it may well be worth investing in a more expensive one that's built to last and fulfills your every need.

• **How big is your garden, and how much storage space do you have?** If you have a small yard, then a small, portable barbecue that can be put away may be the best choice. If you have a bigger garden, then a built-in barbecue can make a great focal point for entertaining and saves the effort of setting up and packing away. If you go for a portable barbecue, check that you have somewhere to store it when it's not in use.

• **How many people will you usually need to cook for?** If you mainly cater for large numbers, then a barbecue with lots of cooking space will be invaluable. However, if you usually cook for just a few people, then a smaller barbecue is more appropriate.

• **Where and when do you want to use it?** Barbecues are great at home, but it can also be fun to take your barbecue on vacation, on a picnic, or to the beach. If this sounds like you, then a small, lightweight, easily portable barbecue might be just the thing.

THE BASIC MODELS

There are five main types of barbecue to choose from, and these can vary considerably in size, shape, cost, and the fuel they use. Look for models with an adjustable grill rack so you can control the heat more easily.

• **Simple braziers** The simplest type of barbecue available, these consist of a tray on legs in which to place the fuel, with a rack over the top for grilling. They may be near to the ground or high enough to stand over while you cook.

• **Kettle barbecues** These round barbecues have a domed lid, which makes them good for both grilling and roasting. They are good for cooking large pieces of meat or whole fish. There are gas-fueled and charcoal-burning models.

• **Built-in barbecues** Usually made of brick, these may be freestanding or built into a walled area. Some have a chimney to carry smoke away from the cooking area.

• **Gas barbecues** These are usually constructed like a cart, with a space for the gas bottle, accessories, and work surface. Gas jets heat up ceramic or lava stones in the base of the barbecue, which then throw out heat to cook the food. Look for models with an easy-to-remove tray for catching dripping fat.

• **Disposable barbecues** Cheap to buy for a one-off barbecue, these usually consist of a sturdy foil tray covered with a lightweight rack—with the charcoal already set up for lighting. Once used, they can simply be left to cool and then be thrown away. They are convenient for picnics or camping, and are also useful if you find you need extra grill-space for a large party, or if you are cooking meat and vegetarian foods that need to be kept separate. However, if you plan to use them frequently, it's cheaper to buy a small, lightweight portable brazier.

Barbecue basics

Once you've chosen your barbecue, all you need to do is find the right position, decide which fuel to use, learn how to light it, and then get the coals (or gas) to just the right temperature before you start cooking.

THE PERFECT POSITION

Before you light the barbecue, think carefully about where to put it. The position should be safe, sensible, stable, and legal.

• **Think about smoke**: don't place the barbecue too close to your house (or your neighbors') or upwind from the eating area.

• **Think about fire**: place the barbecue away from dry plants or wooden fences.

• **Be sure the barbecue is stable** and there is no risk of it getting knocked over.

• **If you are in a public place** check that you are allowed to light a barbecue there.

CHARCOAL, WOOD, OR GAS?

Everyone has their own preference for the perfect fuel—and often the type of barbecue you have will dictate which fuel you choose.

• **Charcoal** is cheap and readily available and burns fairly evenly. It comes in two forms: lumpwood or briquettes. Lumpwood charcoal is easier to light than briquettes. Both can be bought in sacks, or in self-lighting packages.

BARBECUE SAFETY

As with any kind of fire, you need to take care. The following should help you avoid injury or accident:

• Always have a bucket of water to hand to douse or put out flames.
• Make sure the barbecue is stable and in a sensible position before you light it.
• Never use flammable liquids to light a barbecue, or to help it burn.
• Never leave a barbecue unattended.
• Keep children and pets well away from the barbecue.
• Never cook in bare feet.
• Leave the barbecue to cool completely before moving it or removing the grill for cleaning. (Remember that if a barbecue rests on the ground, the ground beneath it will become hot too—so take care when you move the barbecue.)

• **Wood** is less predictable to use and it is more difficult to control the heat. You also need to wait for the fuel to burn down to its glowing embers before you can start cooking.

• **Gas** is quick and convenient but does not offer the same flavor as charcoal or wood.

GETTING FIRED UP

With the help of firelighters and/or matches, lighting a barbecue and getting it to just the right temperature is an easy task.

Charcoal: Start at least 30 minutes before you want to start cooking. If you don't have self-lighting bags of charcoal, the easiest way to get the charcoal burning is by using firelighters. Layer the charcoal with firelighters and build a cone-shaped fire in the center of the barbecue tray. Light the firelighters using a long match, and leave the coals to burn down to ash-coated embers. Spread out the glowing embers into an even layer, then place the grill rack above them and leave it to heat up. If you need to add more coals, add them around the edge of the embers until they warm up, then move them, a few at a time, into the center of the fire. There should be no flames when you start to cook.

Wood: Start about 1 hour before you want to start cooking, then light the wood in the same way as you would charcoal.

Gas: Start about 15 minutes before you want to start cooking. Switch on the gas and light it, then leave the ceramic or lava rocks to heat up.

BARBECUE TOOLS

A few basic tools and accessories will take all the hassle out of cooking on a barbecue. Make sure you've got everything you need before you start putting food on the grill:

- **Long-handled tongs** for turning and lifting food. (Get a second pair for moving coals.)
- **Barbecue trays** for food that is too fragile or too small to cook on the grill.
- **Hinged baskets** for grilling whole fish.
- **Spatula** for turning fish, burgers, and vegetables.
- **Long-pronged fork** for checking that meat and poultry are cooked at the end of cooking. (Avoid piercing uncooked foods because the juices will run out during cooking, giving dry results.)
- **Pastry brush** for basting food and oiling the grill. (Keep a separate brush for basting raw foods.)
- **Metal and wooden skewers** for making kebabs. (Soak wooden skewers in water for at least 30 minutes before use.)
- **Foil** for wrapping foods before cooking.
- **Wire brush** for cleaning the grill rack.

PERFECT BARBECUING

Before you start cooking, oil the grill rack using oiled paper towels or a basting brush. Cooking times can vary considerably, depending on the heat of the coals, the distance of the rack from the heat, and the thickness of the food. However, you can use the following list as a general guideline to how many minutes are needed:

Steaks—*rare:* 3–4; *medium:* 5–6; *well-done:* 8–12
Lamb—*steaks:* 6–8; *chops:* 8
Pork—*chops:* 20; *ribs:* 15; *sausages:* 15
Burgers—*thin:* 8–10; *thick:* 12–15
Chicken—*wings:* 8–10; *breasts:* 12; *thighs:* 20; *legs:* 25
Fish fillets—*thin:* 2; *thick:* 6–7
Whole fish—*small:* 6; *medium:* 15; *large:* up to 1 hour (with lid)
Shellfish: *shrimp:* 4; *scallops/squid:* 2–3

To assess how hot the coals are, hold your hand a few inches above them, and see how long you can keep your hand there:
2 seconds = hot; 3–4 seconds = medium;
5 seconds = low

Fabulous food

The best thing about a barbecue is that almost everything, apart from the actual cooking, can be done in advance. Before you plan the menu, think about the following:

• **How many people have you invited?** This will guide you to the quantity of food and drink needed, and also how many sets of plates, flatware, and glasses you will need. Check that you have enough grill space and fuel to cook the food.

• **Does anyone have special dietary requirements?** If you are catering for a vegetarian or someone with a food allergy, think about whether you will need a separate grill area for their food.

• **How much time do you have for preparation?** This will help you assess the types and numbers of dishes you should prepare. If you're short of time, it might be better to go for a few, simple dishes, whereas if you have a whole day to prepare, you might like to make a number of more complex dishes as well as an impressive dessert.

WHAT KIND OF DISHES?

There's a huge range of delicacies you can cook over a barbecue, from the simplest ready-made sausages and burgers to marinated meat, poultry, and fish, and

mouth-watering vegetarian temptations. You can even barbecue fruits and other sweet foods to make irresistible desserts. (Just flick through the recipes in this book and you'll see how many fabulous ideas there are!)

For a big party, it's great to barbecue a selection of different foods, but you can also cook just one deliciously prepared dish, such as grilled Italian lamb with rosemary oil or stuffed angler fish with balsamic dressing, to great effect. Whatever you decide on, always make a couple of salads and side dishes to accompany the barbecued food, and make sure there's a dessert to follow.

To ensure things run smoothly, offer guests snacks and nibbles while the food cooks. This way, even if you have to wait until the coals are just the right temperature, or the food takes a little longer than expected—your guests won't get hungry or impatient!

CLASSIC GRILLS

Many ingredients can go straight on the grill, while others require a little preparation. Here are just a few of the classic approaches:

• **Straight to the grill** Burgers, sausages, and many cuts of meat, poultry, and fish can go straight on the grill and are good served with tangy sauces, relishes, or salsas (see pages 13–14). Plain grilled fish is often good served with a simple squeeze of lemon juice, or a little garlic or mixed herb butter (see page 15).

• **Marinades and rubs** Meat, poultry, fish, vegetables, and other vegetarian foods such as tofu can be given a real flavor boost with a simple marinade (see page 12). Whether it's chunky steaks, delicate shellfish, or bite-size vegetables, marinating for even a short time can transform them.

• **Sizzling kebabs** Cubes of marinated meat, poultry, fish, vegetables, and other vegetarian ingredients are delicious threaded onto skewers to make kebabs, and they can be made well in advance. Sweet ingredients such as fruit and marshmallows can also be skewered and grilled to make delicious desserts. Woody herbs and aromatics such as rosemary and lemon grass can be used as skewers to impart extra flavor.

• **Tasty parcels** Both sweet and savory ingredients can be wrapped up in foil or banana leaves with flavorings, then cooked over the hot coals to give fabulous results.

• **Stuffed and grilled** Ingredients such as veal escalopes and chunky angler fish can be stuffed with a filling, then tied up to make a parcel. These dishes can make an impressive centerpiece for a sophisticated barbecue.

CREATING AN INSTANT BARBECUE

Even with barely an hour or two to prepare, you can still put on a veritable feast if you choose the right dishes. Here are a few ideas for a super-speedy barbecue:

• Offer guests no-fuss nibbles such as chips and dips when they arrive.
• Go for ready-to-cook and ready-prepared foods such as sausages, burgers, chicken legs or wings, or cubed meat that can quickly be slipped onto skewers with a few bite-size vegetables.
• Use marinades and spice rubs to add quick-fix flavor. They can be put together in seconds, then left to work their magic.
• Make a no-fuss green salad with prepared salad leaves, cucumber, and a splash of ready-made dressing.
• For an almost-instant pasta salad, toss cooked pasta with a jar of marinated vegetables or Italian antipasti. (Drain the vegetables if they're in oil.)
• For a super-speedy potato salad, boil new potatoes until tender, then drain and leave to cool before tossing with mayonnaise, a handful of chopped fresh herbs, and a couple of chopped scallions.
• Buy ready-made sauces and relishes and simply spoon them into serving dishes.
• Don't worry about making a dessert—ice cream or sorbet served with fresh summer berries is a great standby.

Marinades and more

Barbecue marinade

serves **6**
preparation time **5 minutes**

1 teaspoon powdered mustard
1 teaspoon salt
½ teaspoon chili powder
1 tablespoon firmly packed dark
  brown sugar
10 oz can condensed tomato soup
2 tablespoons vinegar
2 tablespoons Worcestershire sauce
2 tablespoons soy sauce

1 Mix all the marinade ingredients together and pour over ribs, chops, or chicken to cover. Leave in a cool place to marinate for at least 1–2 hours.

Herb marinade

serves **4**
preparation time **5 minutes**

4 tablespoons olive oil
4 garlic cloves, crushed
½ cup dry white wine
1 small onion, finely chopped
1 sprig each rosemary, thyme, and parsley

1 Mix all the ingredients together and use to marinate fish, such as tuna or mackerel, for several hours or overnight.

Sweet and sour marinade

serves **4**
preparation time **5 minutes**

4 tablespoons tomato ketchup
2 tablespoons Worcestershire sauce
2 tablespoons white wine vinegar
2 tablespoons honey
2 tablespoons brown sugar

1 Mix together all the ingredients. Place the food in a shallow dish and brush with the marinade, then cover and refrigerate for 4 hours, or preferably overnight. This marinade is perfect for pork spareribs.

Teriyaki marinade

serves **4**
preparation time **5 minutes**

¾ inch piece of fresh ginger root,
  peeled and finely grated
2 tablespoons soy sauce
1 tablespoon lemon juice
2 tablespoons dry sherry
½ cup fish stock

1 In a shallow dish combine all the ingredients for the marinade. Marinate the food for at least 30 minutes, turning occasionally. This is a good marinade for chicken, salmon, and shrimp.

Corn relish

serves **8–10**
preparation time **15 minutes**
cooking time **30 minutes**

4 tablespoons corn oil
2 large onions, finely chopped
1 green bell pepper, cored, seeded, and
  finely chopped
1 red bell pepper, cored, seeded, and
  finely chopped
4 celery sticks, finely chopped
1 teaspoon salt
1 large garlic clove, crushed
2 carrots, peeled and cut into small cubes
¼ cup sugar
2 teaspoons powdered mustard
4 cups frozen corn
1¾ cups vinegar

1 Heat the oil in a large pan and add the onions, peppers, and celery. Fry them until they are soft but not browned, then add the salt and garlic.

2 Add all the remaining ingredients to the pan and bring the mixture to a boil. Reduce the heat and cook, uncovered, for 15 minutes, stirring occasionally.

3 Transfer the relish to a bowl and cool at room temperature. This relish does not need time to mature, but if not immediately consumed, label and store in a cool, dark place for up to 6 months.

Chermoula

serves **6**
preparation time **10 minutes**

2 teaspoons cumin seeds
1 teaspoon coriander seeds
½ teaspoon crushed red pepper
3 garlic cloves, crushed
finely grated zest and juice of 1 lime
3 tablespoons olive oil
1 tablespoon chopped mixed cilantro
  leaves and parsley
1 teaspoon salt

1 Lightly pound the cumin and coriander seeds using a mortar and pestle (or a small bowl and the end of a rolling pin). Mix in a bowl with the remaining ingredients. Use chermoula to coat fish before barbecuing.

Basic tomato sauce

serves **4**
preparation time **10 minutes**
cooking time **1 hour**

2 lb fresh ripe tomatoes, quartered
1 onion, finely chopped
2 garlic cloves, chopped
4 basil leaves, bruised
½ cup olive oil

1 Place the tomatoes in a large saucepan with the onion and garlic. Cover the pan, bring to a boil then cook slowly for 25 minutes. Uncover the pan and simmer for another 15–30 minutes to evaporate any extra liquid: the sauce should be quite thick.

2 Puree the sauce in a blender or food processor, then strain it to remove any seeds and skin. Stir in the basil and oil.

Avocado salsa

serves **4**
preparation time **10 minutes**

1 firm, ripe avocado
2 tablespoons lime juice
1 tablespoon finely chopped cilantro leaves
2 scallions, finely sliced
salt and freshly ground black pepper
diced red bell pepper, to garnish

1 Cut lengthwise through the avocado as far as the pit, then gently twist the two halves apart. Remove the pit, peel off the skin, and cut the avocado into ½-inch dice.

2 Place the avocado flesh in a bowl with the lime juice, cilantro, and scallions. Season to taste with salt and pepper and toss lightly to combine. Cover and refrigerate until required. Serve garnished with diced red bell pepper. This tangy salsa makes a great accompaniment to warm dishes, especially as part of a buffet.

Green mayonnaise

serves **6**
preparation time **10 minutes**

3 egg yolks
1 tablespoon finely chopped chives
1 tablespoon finely chopped parsley
1 tablespoon lemon juice
1¼ cups olive oil
salt and freshly ground black pepper

1 Place the egg yolks, herbs, and lemon juice in a blender or food processor and blend for 1–2 minutes. Keeping the motor running, pour in the oil in a very thin stream until it is all incorporated. Add salt and pepper to taste.

Classic vinaigrette

makes **1 cup**
preparation time **5 minutes**

¾ cup olive oil
4 tablespoons white wine vinegar,
   cider vinegar, or tarragon vinegar
1 teaspoon honey
2 tablespoons chopped mixed herbs
   (mint, parsley, chives, thyme)
1 garlic clove, crushed
salt and freshly ground black pepper

1 Beat the oil with the vinegar, honey, herbs, garlic, and salt and pepper to taste until well blended. Alternatively, place all the ingredients in a screw-top jar and shake vigorously to combine well before using.

Mint dressing

makes ½ **cup**
preparation time **5 minutes, plus standing**

6 tablespoons olive oil
2 tablespoons lemon juice
2–3 tablespoons chopped mint
pinch of sugar
salt and freshly ground black pepper

1 Beat the oil with the lemon juice, mint, sugar, and salt and pepper to taste until well blended, or place all the ingredients in a screw-top jar and shake vigorously to combine well.

2 Set aside for at least 15 minutes to allow the flavors to develop, then beat or shake again and test, before using to dress a cold potato salad or a green leaf salad.

Honey dressing

makes ½ **cup**
preparation time **5 minutes**

4 tablespoons lemon juice
2 tablespoons honey
3 tablespoons olive oil
salt and freshly ground black pepper

1 Beat together the lemon juice, honey, olive oil, and salt and pepper to taste until well blended. Alternatively, place all the ingredients in a screw-top jar and shake vigorously to combine well before using to dress green salads.

Mixed herb butter

serves **6**
preparation time **5 minutes,**
plus chilling

⅓ **cup butter**
½ **tablespoon chopped tarragon**
½ **tablespoon chopped chervil**
½ **tablespoon chopped dill weed**
½ **tablespoon chopped chives**
½ **tablespoon chopped mint**
1 **tablespoon lemon juice**
salt and freshly ground black pepper

1 Blend the butter in a blender or food processor, then add the rest of the ingredients and mix well. Alternatively, beat the butter in a bowl until creamy, then add the remaining ingredients and combine them.

2 Roll the butter in waxed paper to form a sausage shape, then chill until firm. This herb butter can be used with either meat or fish.

Spicy peanut sauce

makes ⅔ **cup**
preparation time **10 minutes**
cooking time **2 minutes**

2 oz creamed coconut
4 tablespoons milk
½ small onion, chopped
1 garlic clove, crushed
4 tablespoons smooth peanut butter
1 teaspoon brown sugar
2 teaspoons soy sauce
½ teaspoon ground cumin
½ teaspoon chili powder
salt and freshly ground black pepper

1 Chop the creamed coconut into pieces and place it in a small pan with the milk. Heat gently for about 2 minutes, stirring constantly, until the coconut melts and forms a paste with the milk.

2 Transfer the coconut mixture to a blender or food processor and add all the remaining ingredients. Process until smooth, then transfer to a small bowl. Cover and set aside until required. It is best to make this rich, spicy dressing in advance to allow the flavors to develop before using it.

Poultry and Game

Versatile poultry, well-flavored duck, and robust, meaty venison are naturals for the barbecue grill. Pepped up with Eastern spices, or infused with rich Mediterranean flavors, the recipes in this chapter are sure to tantalize the tastebuds.

serves **8**
preparation time **30 minutes, plus marinating**
cooking time **12–15 minutes**

Chicken tikka kebabs
with naan bread

**3 lb skinless, boneless chicken
breasts, cut into 1 inch
cubes
8 naan breads
lemon or lime wedges,
to garnish**

**marinade
2 onions, roughly chopped
2 inch piece of fresh ginger
root, peeled and roughly
chopped
4 garlic cloves, crushed
1¼ cups plain yogurt
2 red chilies, seeded, and
chopped
1 tablespoon ground
coriander
2 teaspoons ground cumin
1 teaspoon turmeric
8 tablespoons lemon juice
2 teaspoons salt**

1 To make the marinade, combine all the ingredients in a blender or food processor and process until smooth.

2 Place the chicken cubes in a shallow bowl, pour over the marinade, and toss well to coat. Cover the bowl with plastic wrap and allow the chicken to marinate in the refrigerator for 8 hours or overnight.

3 Remove the chicken from the marinade with a slotted spoon and pour the marinade into a pitcher. Thread the chicken onto 16 metal skewers.

4 Cook the kebabs on an oiled barbecue grill over hot coals for 6 minutes on each side, basting frequently with the marinade. Serve the kebabs with warm naan breads and garnish with wedges of lemon or lime.

BARBIE TIP
While the kebabs are cooking, wrap the naan breads in a foil parcel and heat them on the edge of the barbecue grill.

serves **4**
preparation time **25 minutes, plus marinating**
cooking time **11–13 minutes**

Thai chicken skewers
with fiery dipping sauce

4 boneless, skinless chicken breasts, about 5 oz each, cut into thin strips
steamed rice, to serve
cilantro sprigs, to garnish

marinade
4 Kaffir lime leaves, shredded
2 lemon grass stalks, trimmed of outer leaves and thinly sliced
2 garlic cloves, roughly chopped
1 inch piece of fresh ginger root, peeled and finely grated
1 fresh red chili, finely sliced
6 tablespoons groundnut oil
3 tablespoons chopped cilantro leaves
2 tablespoons lime juice
1 tablespoon Thai fish sauce
1 tablespoon light soy sauce

dipping sauce
1 red chili, seeded, and finely chopped
1 Kaffir lime leaf, shredded
¾ cup coconut milk
2 tablespoons smooth peanut butter
1 tablespoon freshly grated ginger root
1 tablespoon Thai red curry paste
½ tablespoon Thai fish sauce
½ tablespoon soy sauce

1 Mix together all the marinade ingredients in a bowl and add the chicken strips. Cover and chill in the refrigerator for at least 2 hours.

2 Meanwhile, make the dipping sauce. Combine all the ingredients in a small saucepan and simmer gently for about 5 minutes. Keep the sauce warm.

3 Remove the strips of chicken from the marinade and thread them onto 8 presoaked wooden skewers in an S-shape. Place on an oiled barbecue grill over medium coals and cook for 6–8 minutes, turning once, until cooked through.

4 Serve the chicken skewers with steamed rice garnished with cilantro sprigs. Place the dipping sauce in a bowl or drizzle it over the chicken.

BARBIE TIP
When using wooden skewers, presoak them in warm water for at least 30 minutes before using, to avoid them burning over the hot coals.

serves **8**
preparation time **20 minutes, plus marinating**
cooking time **15 minutes**

Chicken skewers
with fruit and nut couscous

**2 lb skinless chicken breast
fillets**
4 tablespoons olive oil
4 garlic cloves, crushed
1 teaspoon ground cumin
1 teaspoon ground turmeric
1 teaspoon paprika
4 teaspoons lemon juice

couscous
8 tablespoons olive oil
2 small onions, finely chopped
2 garlic cloves, crushed
**2 teaspoons each ground cumin,
cinnamon, pepper, and ginger**
¾ cup dried dates, chopped
**¾ cup dried apricots, finely
chopped**
**1 cup blanched almonds, toasted
and chopped**
5 cups vegetable stock
2 cups couscous
2 tablespoons lemon juice
**4 tablespoons chopped cilantro
leaves**
**salt and freshly ground black
pepper**

to garnish
seeds from half a pomegranate
lemon wedges
cilantro sprigs

1 Cut the chicken into long thin strips, place them in a shallow dish and add the olive oil, garlic, spices, and lemon juice. Stir well, then cover and allow to marinate for 2 hours. Thread the chicken onto 16 presoaked wooden skewers.

2 To prepare the fruit and nut mixture, heat half of the oil in a saucepan and fry the onions, garlic, and spices for 5 minutes. Stir in the dried fruits and almonds and remove from the heat.

3 Meanwhile, place the couscous in a bowl, pour over the stock, cover with a dish towel, and leave for 8–10 minutes, until the grains are fluffed up and the liquid absorbed. Stir in the remaining oil and the fruit and nut mixture, add the lemon juice and cilantro, and season with salt and pepper to taste.

4 While the couscous is standing, cook the chicken skewers on an oiled barbecue grill over medium coals for 4–5 minutes on each side, until browned and cooked through. Serve with the couscous, garnished with pomegranate seeds, lemon wedges, and cilantro sprigs.

BARBIE TIP
As an alternative, make the kebabs using large shrimp or pieces of vegetable. Marinate and cook in the same way. Shrimp will take only 1–2 minutes on each side.

serves **4**
preparation time **15 minutes, plus marinating**
cooking time **about 15 minutes**

Chicken teriyaki
with onion and pepper

1½ lb chicken breast fillets, cubed
12 scallions, cut into 2 inch lengths
2 red bell peppers, cored, seeded, and cut into chunks
2 tablespoons vegetable oil
plain boiled rice, to serve

sauce
3 tablespoons soy sauce
3 tablespoons honey
3 tablespoons sake or dry sherry
1 garlic clove, crushed
3 slices of fresh ginger root

1 Place all the sauce ingredients in a small saucepan, bring to a boil and simmer for 5 minutes until it has thickened. Meanwhile, divide the chicken, scallions, and red peppers between 8 presoaked wooden skewers and brush with oil.

2 Place the chicken skewers on an oiled barbecue grill over hot coals and cook for 4 minutes on each side, or until cooked through. Brush with the teriyaki sauce and serve on a bed of plain boiled rice, drizzled with more sauce.

BARBIE TIP
Try to use Japanese-brewed soy sauce, rather than Chinese soy sauce, which has a much saltier, less malty, taste.

serves **4**
preparation time **15–20 minutes**
cooking time **about 10 minutes**

Chicken skewers
with avocado and pistachio salad

4 skinless, boneless chicken
  breasts, about 5 oz each
5 tablespoons extra virgin
  olive oil
large pinch of Cajun spice mix
1 large ripe avocado, peeled,
  pitted, and diced
2 tablespoons lime juice
6 tablespoons pistachio nuts,
  roughly chopped
2½ cups mixed salad leaves
small handful of cilantro
  leaves, torn
salt and freshly ground black
  pepper

1 Cut the chicken breasts into cubes and thread these onto 8 presoaked wooden skewers. Drizzle with a little of the oil, sprinkle with Cajun spice mix, and season with salt and pepper. Place the chicken skewers on an oiled barbecue grill over hot coals and cook for 10 minutes, turning once or twice, until browned and cooked through.

2 Meanwhile, place the avocado flesh in a bowl and toss with the lime juice. Add the remaining olive oil and season to taste with salt and pepper. Add the pistachios to the bowl with the salad leaves and torn cilantro leaves. Toss together gently, then spoon onto plates and top with the cooked chicken skewers.

serves **4**
preparation time **5 minutes**
cooking time **20–25 minutes**

Barbecued chicken
with lemon and herb marinade

2 garlic cloves, crushed
grated zest and juice of
  1 lemon
4 thyme sprigs
6 tablespoons olive oil
1 tablespoon honey
1 teaspoon dried oregano
1 teaspoon ground cumin
2 chicken drumsticks
2 chicken thighs
salt and freshly ground
  black pepper

1 Place the garlic, lemon zest, and juice in a bowl. Add the thyme sprigs, oil, honey, oregano, and cumin and season to taste with salt and pepper.

2 Add the chicken portions and stir until well coated.

3 Place the chicken on an oiled barbecue grill and cook over hot coals for 20–25 minutes, turning and basting until browned and cooked through.

BARBIE TIP
Use the same mixture to coat 12 chicken wings, or try turkey portions instead.

serves **8**
preparation time **30 minutes, plus marinating**
cooking time **8–10 minutes**

Cinnamon-spiced chicken wings
with yellow pepper dip

16 large chicken wings
cilantro sprigs, to garnish

marinade
2 garlic cloves
3 inch piece of fresh ginger
  root, peeled and chopped
juice and finely grated zest
  of 4 limes or 2 lemons
4 tablespoons soy sauce
4 tablespoons groundnut oil
4 teaspoons ground cinnamon
2 teaspoons ground turmeric
4 tablespoons honey
1 teaspoon salt

yellow pepper dip
4 yellow bell peppers
8 tablespoons plain yogurt
2 tablespoons soy sauce
2 tablespoons chopped cilantro
  leaves
freshly ground black pepper

1 Place all the marinade ingredients in a blender or food processor and blend until very smooth. Place the chicken in a bowl, pour over the marinade, toss, cover, and allow to marinate for 1–2 hours.

2 To make the yellow pepper dip, place the yellow peppers under a preheated broiler for about 10 minutes, turning until well charred and blistered all over. Place them in a plastic bag until cool, then peel and seed them and place the flesh in a blender or food processor with the yogurt; blend until smooth. Pour into a bowl, add the soy sauce, and season with pepper; stir in the chopped cilantro and set aside.

3 Drain the chicken and cook on an oiled barbecue grill over medium coals for 4–5 minutes on each side, basting with the remaining marinade. Garnish with cilantro sprigs and serve with the dip.

> **BARBIE TIP**
> Because the chicken wings are quite small, you can get plenty of them on the barbecue grill at the same time, which makes them great for large parties.

serves **4**
preparation time **15 minutes, plus marinating**
cooking time **about 25 minutes**

Chargrilled chicken
with cilantro salsa

**4 skinless chicken breast
   fillets, about 7 oz each**

marinade
**2 tablespoons soy sauce
2 teaspoons sesame oil
1 tablespoon olive oil
2 teaspoons honey
pinch of crushed red pepper**

salsa
**1 red onion, diced
1 small garlic clove, crushed
1 bunch of cilantro leaves,
   roughly chopped
6 tablespoons olive oil
grated zest and juice of
   1 lemon
1 teaspoon ground cumin
salt and freshly ground black
   pepper**

to serve
**steamed couscous
diced tomato**

1 Combine the marinade ingredients in a shallow dish, add the chicken fillets, cover, and marinate in the refrigerator for at least 8 hours, but preferably 24 hours.

2 Cook the chicken on an oiled barbecue grill over medium coals for 8 minutes on each side, until browned and cooked through. Wrap them in foil and allow to rest for 5 minutes.

3 Meanwhile, mix all the salsa ingredients together and season with salt and pepper. Set aside to infuse.

4 Strain the marinade juices into a small saucepan and bring to a boil, then remove from the heat but keep warm.

5 Serve the chicken with the couscous tossed with diced tomato and top it with the salsa and the marinade sauce.

BARBIE TIP
To ensure the chicken is chargrilled on the outside but still moist inside, place it on a hot grill and cook over medium coals.

serves **4**
preparation time **10 minutes**
cooking time **20 minutes**

Crispy duck breasts
with orange and cranberry sauce

2 oranges
1 cup cranberries
¼ cup light brown sugar
1 tablespoon honey
4 duck breasts
salt and freshly ground black
  pepper

to serve
mashed potato

1 Remove the rind and pith from the oranges and cut them into segments.

2 Place the orange segments, cranberries, and sugar in a saucepan with salt and pepper to taste, bring to a boil then simmer until the cranberries are soft. Stir in the honey, and keep warm.

3 Place the duck breasts on an oiled barbecue grill, skin side down, and cook over medium coals for 6–10 minutes, then turn them over and cook on the other side for 4–6 minutes. The skin should be crispy and the flesh tender.

4 Cut the duck into slices and serve with the orange and cranberry sauce. Serve with mashed potato, if desired.

serves **4–6**
preparation time **15 minutes, plus marinating**
cooking time **20 minutes**

Chicken drumsticks
with Jamaican jerk marinade

2 tablespoons sunflower oil
1 small onion, finely chopped
10 allspice berries
2 hot red chilies, seeded and
roughly chopped
3 tablespoons lime juice
1 teaspoon salt
12 chicken drumsticks

1 Place all the ingredients, except the chicken drumsticks, in a food processor or spice mill and grind to a paste.

2 Score the chicken drumsticks deeply with a sharp-pointed knife, cutting right down as far as the bone.

3 Coat the chicken with the jerk seasoning mixture, brushing it into the slashes in the meat so that the flavor will penetrate. Cover and marinate in the refrigerator overnight.

4 Place the drumsticks on an oiled barbecue grill over hot coals. Cook, turning frequently, for about 20 minutes, or until the chicken is brown on the outside and no longer pink on the inside. Serve hot, warm or cold, for people to eat with their fingers.

BARBIE TIP
Jerk seasoning can be used with other cuts of chicken, such as thighs or breasts. It is also very good with pork; indeed, jerk pork is one of Jamaica's most famous national dishes.

serves **4**
preparation time **20 minutes**
cooking time **20–25 minutes**

Turkey, tomato, and tarragon burgers
with pancetta

**8 sun-dried tomato halves
in oil, drained and chopped**
1 lb ground turkey
**1 tablespoon chopped
tarragon**
½ red onion, finely chopped
½ teaspoon paprika
½ teaspoon salt
**4 slices smoked pancetta
or rindless bacon, halved**

to serve
4 ciabatta rolls
**shredded radicchio and
crisp lettuce**

1 Place the sun-dried tomatoes, turkey, and tarragon in a blender or food processor and process until smooth. Spoon the mixture into a bowl and stir in the onion. Season with the paprika and salt. Mix well, divide into 4, and shape into burgers. Stretch 2 strips of pancetta over each burger and secure the pancetta with toothpicks.

2 Barbecue the burgers over hot coals for 20–25 minutes, turning frequently. Serve at once in the ciabatta rolls with shredded radicchio and lettuce.

BARBIE TIP
Soak the toothpicks
in water for 30 minutes
before use, as you would
with wooden skewers, to
prevent them burning
during cooking.

serves **4**
preparation time **10 minutes**
cooking time **up to 45 minutes**

Loin of venison
with pepper crust

1½ lb loin of venison, cut from the haunch
3 tablespoons mixed peppercorns, crushed
1 tablespoon juniper berries, crushed
½ teaspoon salt
1 egg white, lightly beaten

to serve
green beans
red currant jelly
sweet potato fries (optional)

1 Make sure that the venison fits on your barbecue grill; if necessary, cut the loin in half to fit.

2 Mix together the peppercorns, juniper berries, and salt, and place in a large shallow dish. Dip the venison into the egg white, then roll it in the peppercorn mixture, covering it evenly all over.

3 Cook the venison on an oiled barbecue grill over hot coals for 4 minutes on each side, turning it carefully so that the crust stays intact. Cook it evenly on all sides, then transfer the loin to a lightly greased roasting pan and cook in a preheated oven, 400°F, for another 15 minutes for rare, and up to 30 minutes for well done. The exact time depends on the thickness of the loin of venison.

4 Let the venison rest for a few minutes, then slice thickly and serve with green beans, red currant jelly, and finely sliced sweet potato fries, if desired.

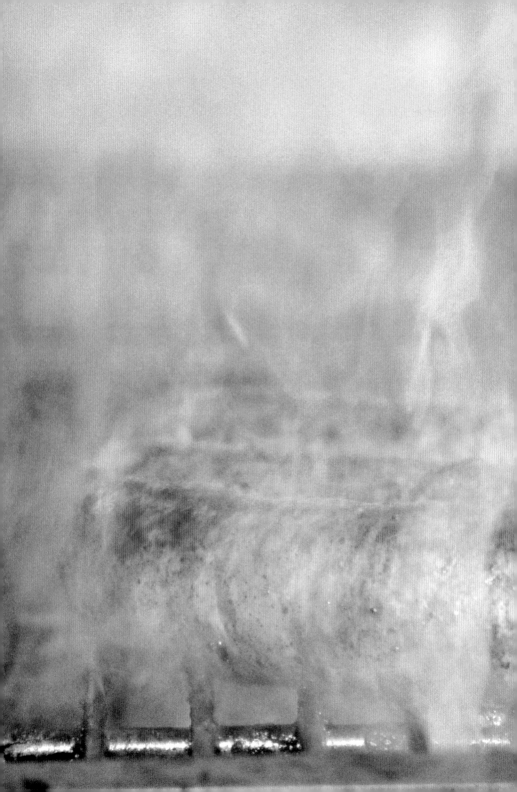

Meat

Sizzling steaks, spicy burgers, sticky spareribs, and juicy lamb chops are all classics for the barbecue grill. Whether it's a laid-back barbecue for a Sunday afternoon, or a sophisticated *al fresco* dinner, you're sure to find the perfect recipe among these pages.

serves **2**
preparation time **15 minutes, plus cooling and marinating**
cooking time **about 30 minutes**

Sweet sticky spareribs
with spicy marinade

1 side pork spareribs, about
   1½ lb

marinade
1 small onion, finely chopped
1 garlic clove, crushed
1 inch piece of fresh ginger
   root, peeled and freshly
   grated
⅓ cup cider vinegar
⅓ cup cola-flavored drink
2 tablespoons tomato
   ketchup
1 tablespoon Worcestershire
   sauce
1 tablespoon dark brown
   sugar
1 tablespoon maple syrup
½ teaspoon Tabasco sauce
½ teaspoon smoked sweet
   paprika
½ teaspoon oregano
½ teaspoon ground cumin
½ teaspoon ground coriander
salt and freshly ground
   black pepper

to serve
baked potatoes
homemade coleslaw

1 Place all the marinade ingredients in a small saucepan and heat slowly until just boiling. Reduce the heat and simmer gently for 8–10 minutes, then set aside to cool.

2 Cut the side of pork ribs into 4 pieces and arrange in a large, shallow dish. Pour over the cold marinade, making sure the pork is well coated. Cover and refrigerate for 12 hours or overnight.

3 Place the ribs on an oiled barbecue grill over hot coals. Cook the ribs for about 20 minutes, turning occasionally, until cooked through and sticky. While they are cooking, place the remaining marinade in a small pan on the stovetop and simmer gently for 10–15 minutes until thick and glossy.

4 Separate the ribs and serve with baked potatoes, homemade coleslaw, and the hot marinade.

serves **4**
preparation time **25 minutes**
cooking time **20 minutes**

Pork, prune, and leek sausages
with barbecued tomatoes

**1 leek, about 5 oz, rinsed
   and diced
12 oz lean ground pork
¼ cup millet flakes
⅔ cup ready-to-eat pitted
   prunes, chopped
1 egg yolk
large pinch of ground nutmeg
4 tomatoes, halved
salt and freshly ground
   black pepper
sweet potato mash, to serve**

1 Cook the leeks in the top of a steamer for 3 minutes until just tender.

2 Mix the ground pork in a bowl with the millet flakes, prunes, egg yolk, nutmeg, and a little salt and pepper, then stir in the leeks.

3 Spoon the mixture into 8 equal mounds on a cutting board then shape each one into a 4 inch long sausage with wetted hands, and place on a barbecue pan.

4 Place the pan on the barbecue grill, and cook for 10 minutes over medium coals, turning the sausages occasionally. Add the tomatoes to the pan and cook for 10 more minutes, until the sausages are golden and the tomatoes hot. Spoon onto plates and serve with sweet potato mash.

BARBIE TIP
Using millet flakes instead of bread crumbs means that even those people on a gluten-free diet can enjoy a sausage supper. Experiment with your own flavor combinations or add a little crushed juniper, chili, or garlic instead of the nutmeg.

serves **4**
preparation time **15–20 minutes**
cooking time **4–5 minutes**

Veal scallops
with artichoke paste

**4 oz bottled globe artichokes
in oil, drained, 1 tablespoon
oil reserved**
**4 sun-dried tomato halves in
oil, drained**
**4 veal scallops, about 4 oz
each**
2 slices prosciutto, halved
4 small mozzarella balls
sunflower oil
**salt and freshly ground black
pepper**
scallions, to garnish (optional)

1 Place the artichokes, the reserved oil, and sun-dried tomatoes in a blender or food processor and process to a smooth paste. Transfer to a bowl and season to taste with salt and pepper.

2 Lay the scallops between two sheets of lightly oiled plastic wrap and pound them with a meat mallet until they are thin but not broken.

3 Spread each scallop with a quarter of the artichoke paste, top with half a slice of prosciutto and a mozzarella ball. Fold the veal over to make a parcel and seal at each end with a toothpick.

4 Brush the parcels with oil. Cook on an oiled barbecue grill over hot coals for 4–5 minutes, turning frequently, until the meat is well cooked. Remove the toothpicks if you desire and serve immediately. If you like, garnish with scallions that have been barbecued for a few seconds until wilted.

BARBIE TIP
If you cannot find small mozzarella balls, cut a whole mozzarella cheese into four.

serves **4**
preparation time **10 minutes**
cooking time **about 10 minutes**

Steak and feta burgers
with sun-dried tomatoes

1 lb ground steak
1 tablespoon sun-dried
tomato paste
2 teaspoons chopped oregano
2 oz feta cheese, crumbled
1 egg, beaten
4 whole-wheat rolls, toasted
1 red onion, sliced
1 small, firm lettuce, leaves
separated
freshly ground black pepper

1 In a large bowl, mix together the ground steak, tomato paste, oregano, and feta. Season well with pepper, and stir through enough beaten egg to bind. Form the mixture into 4 burgers.

2 Place the burgers on an oiled barbecue grill over hot coals and cook for 4–5 minutes on each side, or until browned and cooked through. Make up the burgers in the rolls using the onion and lettuce, and serve with a napkin.

serves **4**
preparation time **10 minutes**
cooking time **6–14 minutes**

Red-hot hamburgers
with spicy greens

1¼ lb ground beef
2 garlic cloves, crushed
1 red onion, finely chopped
1 red chili, finely chopped
1 bunch of parsley, chopped
1 tablespoon Worcestershire
   sauce
1 egg, beaten
4 white or whole-wheat
   hamburger buns, split
spicy greens, such as arugula
   or mizuna
1 beefsteak tomato, sliced
salt and freshly ground black
   pepper
corn relish, to serve (see
   page 13)

1 Place the ground beef in a large bowl. Add the garlic, red onion, red chili, parsley, Worcestershire sauce, beaten egg, and a little salt and pepper. Mix well.

2 Divide the beef mixture into 4 equal amounts and shape into burgers. Place the burgers on the barbecue grill and cook over hot coals for 3 minutes on each side for rare, 5 minutes for medium, or 7 minutes for well done.

3 Toast the bun halves quickly on a clean, hot grill. Fill each bun with some greens, sliced tomato, and a grilled burger. Serve with some corn relish.

BARBIE TIP
These burgers can also be made with ground lamb and served in pita breads, if preferred.

serves **4**
preparation time **25 minutes, plus cooling and chilling**
cooking time **30–35 minutes**

Beef satay
with Indonesian peanut dipping sauce

1 lb beef sirloin steak

marinade
6 tablespoons coconut milk
2 tablespoons soy sauce
1 red chili, finely chopped
2 garlic cloves, crushed
grated zest and juice of 1 lime
lime zest, to garnish

Indonesian peanut dipping
sauce
2 tablespoons sunflower oil
1 small onion, finely grated
2 garlic cloves, crushed
1 inch piece of fresh ginger
   root, peeled and grated
¼ cup dry roasted peanuts,
   ground in a blender or
   nut mill
large pinch of hot chili
   powder
½ teaspoon soy sauce
2 tablespoons crunchy
   peanut butter
1–2 tablespoons dark brown
   sugar
2 tablespoons lime juice
¾ cup coconut cream

to serve
crisp green salad leaves

1 Cut the beef lengthwise into thin strips. Place all the marinade ingredients in a bowl and mix together. Add the beef strips and turn to coat well. Cover and allow to marinate in the refrigerator for at least 4 hours.

2 To make the sauce, heat the oil in a saucepan and gently fry the onion, garlic, ginger, and ground peanuts for 10 minutes to develop the flavors. Add the chili powder, soy sauce, peanut butter, sugar, lime juice, and coconut cream, stirring well to combine them. Bring to a boil, then reduce the heat and cook gently for another 10 minutes.

3 Transfer the sauce to a bowl and allow to cool, then cover and chill for at least 30 minutes.

4 Drain the beef, keeping the marinade to one side, then thread the beef in a zig-zag pattern onto 8 presoaked wooden skewers. Place the skewers on a lightly oiled barbecue grill and cook over hot coals for 7–8 minutes, or until they are cooked through, turning them and brushing over a little of the marinade from time to time while they are cooking. Serve the beef strips on crisp green salad leaves with some peanut dipping sauce and garnish with strips of lime zest.

BARBIE TIP
In this recipe, the sauce is thicker and richer than the usual satay sauce, so it can be used as a dip. It is delicious with chunky pieces of grilled vegetables and grilled skewered meats, particularly chicken.

serves **4**
preparation time **5 minutes, plus marinating**
cooking time **6–24 minutes**

Sirloin steak
with teriyaki marinade

1½ lb thick-cut sirloin steak
stir-fried noodles and
  vegetables, to serve

teriyaki marinade
6 tablespoons pineapple juice
4 tablespoons soy sauce
2 garlic cloves, crushed
1¼ inch piece of fresh ginger
  root, peeled and finely
  chopped

1 Mix together all the ingredients for the marinade. Place the sirloin steak in a shallow dish and cover with the marinade. Turn the steak to coat it well. Cover and refrigerate for 24 hours, turning the meat as frequently as possible.

2 Cook the steak on an oiled barbecue grill over hot coals for 3–4 minutes on each side for rare, 5–6 minutes for medium, or 8–12 minutes for well done. Remove when the meat is cooked to your desire.

3 Allow the meat to rest for a few minutes, then slice it thinly. Serve on a bed of stir-fried noodles and vegetables.

BARBIE TIP
Teriyaki is a popular Japanese marinade. The complex flavors of soy sauce and ginger penetrate the meat with very tasty results.

serves **2**
preparation time **30 minutes, plus chilling**
cooking time **15–20 minutes**

Lamb and red bean koftas
with cucumber relish

1 small onion
1 garlic clove, chopped
8 oz lean ground lamb
7 oz can red kidney beans,
  drained and rinsed
¼ teaspoon ground allspice
3 tablespoons fresh bread
  crumbs
1 egg yolk
12–16 bay leaves, depending
  on size
olive oil
salt and freshly ground black
  pepper

cucumber relish
2 inch piece of cucumber,
  diced
1 kiwifruit, diced
1 tablespoon chopped mint
few flakes of crushed red
  pepper (optional)

to serve
4 pita breads
shredded lettuce
plain yogurt

1 To make the koftas place all the ingredients, except the bay leaves and oil, in a food processor. Season with salt and pepper and blend together. With damp hands, shape into 20 small balls and thread onto 4 metal or presoaked wooden skewers. Place on a baking sheet, tuck the bay leaves underneath and between the meatballs, and loosely cover with plastic wrap, then refrigerate.

2 Mix together the relish ingredients in a small bowl, cover with plastic wrap, and refrigerate until required. Brush the koftas with oil and cook on a barbecue grill over hot coals for 12–15 minutes, turning occasionally, until they are browned and cooked through.

3 Sprinkle the pita breads with water and heat on the barbecue grill until puffy. Make a cut lengthwise in the pitas and, discarding the bay leaves, fill with the koftas, lettuce, relish, and some yogurt, to serve.

makes **12**
preparation time **10 minutes, plus chilling (optional)**
cooking time **10 minutes**

Sheekh kebabs
with red onions

2 **green chilies, seeded, and**
finely chopped
1 **teaspoon grated fresh**
ginger root
2 **garlic cloves, crushed**
3 **tablespoons chopped**
cilantro leaves
2 **tablespoons chopped mint**
leaves
1 **teaspoon cumin seeds**
1 **tablespoon vegetable oil**
½ **teaspoon ground cloves**
½ **teaspoon ground cardamom**
1 **lb ground lamb**
salt

to garnish
mint sprigs
lemon wedges

to serve
French bread
red onion, sliced

1 Place the chilies, ginger, garlic, cilantro, mint, cumin, oil, ground cloves, and cardamom in a food processor or blender and process until fairly smooth. Transfer to a mixing bowl, add the lamb, season with salt and mix well, using your hands. Divide the mixture into 12 portions, then cover and chill for 30 minutes, if time allows.

2 Lightly oil 12 flat metal skewers and mold a sausage-shaped portion of the kebab mixture around each skewer.

3 Place the kebabs on an oiled barbecue grill over hot coals and cook for 3–4 minutes on each side, or until cooked through and browned. Meanwhile, cut diagonal slices from the French loaf and place them on the barbecue grill; cook, turning over halfway, until brown and crispy.

4 Serve the kebabs with the hot French bread and slices of red onion and garnish with mint sprigs and lemon wedges.

BARBIE TIP

The meat mixture can also be formed into balls and threaded on the skewers, perhaps alternating the meatballs with pieces of onion or bell pepper.

serves **4**
preparation time **20 minutes**
cooking time **10–20 minutes**

Grilled Italian lamb
with rosemary oil

**lamb loin roast, about 1½ lb,
trimmed of fat
4 garlic cloves, cut into slivers
few small rosemary sprigs
2 red onions, quartered
4 tablespoons olive oil
1 tablespoon chopped
rosemary
salt and freshly ground black
pepper**

**to serve
fresh pasta
Parmesan cheese shavings**

1 Make small incisions all over the loin roast and insert the garlic slivers and rosemary sprigs. Place the lamb on an oiled barbecue grill and cook over medium coals, turning occasionally, until browned all over, for about 10 minutes for rare meat, or about 20 minutes for well done. Add the onions to the grill for the last 10 minutes and char on the outside. Let the lamb rest for 5 minutes, then carve into slices.

2 Meanwhile, place the oil and the chopped rosemary in a mortar and crush with a pestle to release the flavors. Season with salt and pepper. Spoon the rosemary oil over the lamb slices and serve at once with the grilled onions. Serve with fresh pasta, lightly tossed in olive oil, and Parmesan shavings.

serves **4**
preparation time **5 minutes, plus marinating**
cooking time **about 1–1¼ hours**

Rosemary and lemon lamb chops
with sweet potato skins

4 sweet potatoes
juice and finely grated zest
   of ½ lemon
1 garlic clove, crushed
4 rosemary sprigs, finely
   chopped
4 anchovy fillets in oil,
   drained and finely chopped
2 tablespoons olive oil
2 tablespoons lemon cordial
12 lamb rib chops
salt and freshly ground black
   pepper
arugula leaves, to garnish

1 Bake the sweet potatoes in a preheated oven, 375°F, for 45–60 minutes until soft right through. Meanwhile, place the lemon zest and juice in a bowl and add the garlic, rosemary, anchovies, olive oil, and lemon cordial. Mix thoroughly and add the lamb chops. Season with salt and pepper, turn to coat, and set aside to marinate for 15 minutes.

2 Cut the sweet potatoes into quarters, scoop out some of the flesh, brush the skins with oil, and season with salt and pepper.

3 Place the lamb and potato skins on an oiled barbecue grill over hot coals, and cook for 3–5 minutes on each side, until the lamb is browned and cooked through. Allow to rest for a few minutes, then serve garnished with arugula leaves.

BARBIE TIP
Trim as much fat as possible off the lamb before cooking. Excess fat will drip down onto the coals and cause flare-ups and burnt food.

MEAT **51**

serves **6–8**
preparation time **30 minutes, plus soaking**
cooking time **2 hours**

Butterflied leg of lamb
with flageolets and garlic

1¼ cups dried flageolet beans or navy beans
2 bay leaves
1 large leg of lamb (approx. 4 lb), boned and butterflied
3 tablespoons olive oil
4 whole garlic bulbs
2 tablespoons butter
1 large onion
6 celery sticks, cut into ½ inch pieces
½ cup mint or parsley leaves
salt and freshly ground black pepper
crusty bread, to serve

1 Place the beans in a bowl with cold water to cover. Soak overnight, then drain, rinse, and drain again. Tip the beans into a large saucepan, add the bay leaves, and cover with cold water. Bring to a boil, boil rapidly for about 10 minutes, then lower the heat and simmer gently for 50–60 minutes until just tender. Drain the beans well, discarding the bay leaves, then set aside.

2 Remove most of the skin and fat from the lamb, leaving only a thin layer. Brush with the oil and place flat on an oiled barbecue grill over hot coals. Sear the meat for 5–6 minutes on each side, then turn and cook for 10–15 minutes more on each side. About 8–10 minutes before the end of the cooking time, wrap each garlic bulb in a double thickness of foil and place in the embers of the fire to soften the flesh.

3 When the meat is thoroughly cooked, transfer it to a platter, cover with a tent of foil, and allow to rest for 10 minutes. Meanwhile, melt the butter in a large saucepan. Add the onion and celery and cook gently for 10–12 minutes, until softened but not browned. Add the flageolet or navy beans and heat through, stirring occasionally. Season to taste with salt and pepper, remove from the heat, and toss with the mint or parsley leaves.

4 Slice the lamb and serve with the beans. Add some roasted garlic to each portion and offer plenty of crusty bread.

BARBIE TIP
An easy way to barbecue a whole joint like lamb is to remove the bone and flatten it; this speeds up the cooking process. You could do this yourself, or ask your butcher to do it for you.

Fish and Shellfish

Nothing could be more delicious than fresh fish and shellfish, combined with aromatic flavors and grilled until tender and juicy. Choose fresh sardines, chunky swordfish skewers, or stuffed angler fish fillets to make a truly memorable barbecue.

serves **4**
preparation time **10 minutes**
cooking time **15 minutes**

Barbecued snapper
with carrots and caraway seeds

1 lb carrots, sliced
2 teaspoons caraway seeds
4 snapper fillets, about
6 oz each
2 oranges
1 handful of cilantro leaves,
roughly chopped, plus extra
to garnish
4 tablespoons olive oil
salt and freshly ground black
pepper

1 Place the carrots in a chargrill pan on the stovetop and cook for 3 minutes on each side, adding the caraway seeds for the last 2 minutes of cooking. Transfer to a bowl and keep warm.

2 Cook the snapper fillets on an oiled barbecue grill over medium coals for 3 minutes on each side.

3 Meanwhile, juice one of the oranges and cut the other into quarters. Place the orange quarters on the barbecue grill until browned.

4 Add the cilantro leaves to the carrots and mix well. Season with salt and pepper to taste and stir in the olive oil and orange juice. Serve the cooked fish with the carrots and grilled orange wedges. Garnish with extra chopped cilantro.

serves **2**
preparation time **15 minutes**
cooking time **6–8 minutes**

Fresh sardines
with cilantro and lime sauce

6 fresh sardines, about 1 lb,
   gutted and scaled
2 limes
4 teaspoons olive oil, plus
   extra to grease
¾ cup cilantro leaves, chopped
salt and freshly ground black
   pepper

1 Rinse the fish under cold running water; rub away any remaining scales with your fingertips and check that the insides are clean. Drain the fish, dry them with paper towels and place in a hinged barbecue basket designed for fish.

2 Place the basket on the grill rack over hot coals, and cook the sardines for 3 minutes on each side, until they are golden and the flesh flakes easily when pressed with a knife. Transfer the fish to serving plates.

3 Cut one of the limes into wedges and squeeze the juice from the second. Mix the juice, oil, cilantro leaves, salt, and pepper together and spoon over the sardines. Serve the sardines with the lime wedges.

BARBIE TIP
Sardines are surprisingly cheap to buy and make a nutritious summer supper when served with a green salad and new potatoes.

serves **2**
preparation time **10 minutes**
cooking time **10–15 minutes**

Angler fish brochettes
with cannellini beans and pesto

**8 oz angler fish, cut
into 6 pieces**
6 prosciutto slices
6 cherry tomatoes
**1 yellow bell pepper, cored,
seeded, and cut into
6 pieces**
1 tablespoon olive oil
**10 oz can cannellini beans,
drained and rinsed**
**2 tablespoons ready-made
fresh pesto**

1 Wrap each piece of fish in a slice of prosciutto. Thread onto 2 metal or presoaked wooden skewers, alternating with tomatoes and yellow pepper pieces. Brush the kebabs with the oil and cook on an oiled barbecue grill over hot coals for 3–4 minutes. Turn and cook for an additional 3 minutes until cooked through.

2 Place the beans in a nonstick saucepan and cook, stirring, over a low heat for 4–5 minutes, or until hot. Stir in the pesto. Spoon the beans onto 2 plates, top with the brochettes, and serve immediately.

serves **4**
preparation time **10–15 minutes**
cooking time **20–28 minutes**

Stuffed angler fish
with balsamic dressing

½ cup balsamic vinegar
4 angler fish fillets, about
  5 oz each
4 teaspoons good-quality
  tapenade
8 basil leaves
8 bacon slices, stretched
  with the back of a knife
11 oz green beans
1⅓ cups frozen peas
6 scallions, finely sliced
4 oz feta cheese, crumbled
2 tablespoons basil oil
salt

1 Pour the balsamic vinegar into a small saucepan. Bring to a boil over a medium heat, then simmer for about 8–10 minutes until thick and glossy. Set aside to cool slightly, but keep warm.

2 Place the angler fish fillets on a cutting board and, using a sharp knife, make a deep incision about 2 inches long in the side of each fillet. Stuff with 1 teaspoon tapenade and 2 basil leaves. Wrap 2 strips of bacon around each fillet, sealing in the filling. Fasten with presoaked toothpicks.

3 Bring a saucepan of salted water to a boil, add the green beans and cook for 5 minutes. Add the peas, bring back to a boil and cook for another 3 minutes. Drain and keep warm.

4 Place the angler fish directly on an oiled barbecue grill. Cook over medium coals for 4–5 minutes on each side until the fish are done. Set aside and allow to rest for a minute or two.

5 Meanwhile, toss the beans and peas with the scallions, feta, and basil oil, and arrange on serving plates. Top with an angler fish fillet (toothpicks removed) and serve immediately, drizzled with the warm balsamic dressing.

serves **4**
preparation time **20 minutes, plus marinating**
cooking time **15–20 minutes**

Angler fish fillets
with garlic and rosemary

1 lb ripe tomatoes, skinned
1 tablespoon balsamic vinegar
2 angler fish fillets, about
   12 oz each, skinned
4 garlic cloves, cut into thin
   slivers
2 long rosemary sprigs
5 tablespoons olive oil
1 tablespoon lemon juice
salt and freshly ground black
   pepper
crusty bread, to serve

1 Place the tomatoes in a blender or food processor and process until smooth. Strain through a sieve into a bowl, season to taste with the vinegar, salt, and pepper, then cover and set aside.

2 Slice each fish fillet lengthwise, almost but not quite all the way through, to make a pocket. Lay the garlic slivers down the length of the pocket in each fillet and top with a rosemary sprig. Add salt and pepper to taste. Re-form both fillets and tie them with string at ¾ inch intervals.

3 Mix the olive oil and lemon juice in a shallow dish, large enough to hold both fillets. Add the angler fish, spoon the oil and lemon juice over the top, then cover. Marinate for 1 hour, turning occasionally.

4 Drain the angler fish and cook on an oiled barbecue grill over medium coals for 15–20 minutes, turning and basting frequently, until the flesh is opaque and just cooked. Meanwhile, pour the tomato sauce into a small saucepan and heat through. Remove the string and slice the fish thinly. Serve with the tomato sauce and some good crusty bread.

BARBIE TIP
Rosemary is a very pungent herb. Here, the angler fish fillets are stuffed with sharpened rosemary sprigs with the leaves removed, so the aroma permeates the fish without being overwhelming.

serves **4**
preparation time **20 minutes, plus marinating**
cooking time **5–6 minutes**

Mediterranean swordfish skewers
with peppers and mango

1 lb swordfish steak, skinned
  and cut into large cubes
1 green bell pepper, cored,
  seeded, and cut into 1 inch
  pieces
1 red bell pepper, cored,
  seeded, and cut into 1 inch
  pieces
1 red onion, cut into quarters
1 ripe but firm mango, peeled
  and cut into thick slices

marinade
2–3 thyme sprigs
leaves from 1–2 rosemary
  sprigs
grated zest of 1 lemon
1 garlic clove, lightly crushed
8 tablespoons olive oil
2 teaspoons fennel seeds
freshly ground black pepper

fennel and olive salad
1 large fennel bulb, sliced
  very finely
½ cup good-quality Kalamata
  olives, pitted
grated zest of 1 lemon
2 tablespoons extra virgin
  olive oil
1 tablespoon lemon juice
salt and freshly ground black
  pepper
fennel fronds, to garnish

1 Mix together all the marinade ingredients and place in a large, shallow dish with the swordfish cubes, peppers, onion, and mango. Cover and set aside at room temperature for about 1 hour.

2 Arrange the fennel slices on a large serving plate and sprinkle with the olives and lemon zest.

3 Thread the swordfish, peppers, onion, and mango onto metal or presoaked wooden skewers. Place the skewers directly on the oiled barbecue grill and cook over medium coals for about 5 minutes, turning occasionally, until the fish is thoroughly cooked.

4 Drizzle the olive oil and lemon juice over the fennel salad and sprinkle with the fennel fronds. Season well with salt and pepper and serve immediately with the swordfish skewers.

serves **4**
preparation time **5 minutes, plus chilling**
cooking time **6–8 minutes**

Swordfish steaks
with mustard and chive butter

½ cup butter, softened
2 tablespoons finely snipped
  chives
1 tablespoon prepared
  English mustard
4 swordfish steaks or fillets,
  about 7 oz each
4 tablespoons lemon juice
salt and freshly ground black
  pepper

to garnish
whole chives
lemon wedges

to serve
cherry tomato salad
new potatoes or boiled rice

1 In a small bowl, mix the butter, chives, and mustard. Turn the butter onto a piece of waxed paper and press it into a sausage shape. Wrap the paper around the butter, twist the ends, and roll the butter into a neat sausage, then chill it in the freezer for 10–15 minutes or until firm.

2 Lay the swordfish on an oiled barbecue grill and sprinkle with lemon juice. Season the fish well with salt and pepper and grill over hot coals for 6–8 minutes or until cooked through, when the fish will flake easily.

3 While the fish is grilling, remove the butter from the freezer and cut it into slices. Transfer the fish to warmed serving plates and top with the butter. Garnish with chives and lemon wedges and serve at once. A cherry tomato salad and new potatoes or boiled rice go well with the fish.

BARBIE TIP
Mahi mahi and halibut
are particularly good in
place of the swordfish
as they are also firm
and flavorsome.

serves **4**
preparation time **15 minutes**
cooking time **3–4 minutes, plus resting**

Spiced swordfish
with fennel and mint salad

**2 teaspoons crushed
coriander seeds
4 swordfish steaks, about
7 oz each
4–6 tablespoons extra virgin
olive oil
1 large fennel bulb, trimmed
1 garlic clove, thinly sliced
2 tablespoons baby capers
in salt, rinsed
handful of mint leaves
1–2 tablespoons lemon juice
salt and freshly ground black
pepper
arugula leaves, to serve**

1 Combine the coriander seeds with some salt and pepper. Brush the swordfish fillets with a little of the oil and rub with the spice mix. Set aside until ready to cook.

2 Discard the tough outer layer of fennel, cut the bulb in half lengthwise and then crosswise, into wafer-thin slices. Place in a bowl with the garlic, capers, mint leaves, the remaining oil, and lemon juice. Season with salt and pepper.

3 Cook the swordfish steaks on an oiled barbecue grill over hot coals for 1½ minutes on each side, then wrap them in foil and allow to rest for 5 minutes. Serve the swordfish and any juices with the fennel salad and arugula.

BARBIE TIP
Swordfish is a wonderfully meaty fish that requires only a short cooking time; if you overcook it, it can become dry and tough. As with meat, allowing the fish to rest before eating it maximizes its moistness and tenderness.

serves **4**
preparation time **15 minutes, plus cooling and chilling**
cooking time **20 minutes**

Fresh tuna steaks
with corn and avocado salsa

4 tuna steaks, about
  6 oz each

salsa
2 corn ears, stripped of husks
  and threads
3 tablespoons extra virgin
  olive oil
1 tablespoon finely chopped
  red onion
3–4 tablespoons lime juice
2 dashes of jalapeño sauce
1 small red chili, seeded, and
  finely chopped
¼ small red bell pepper,
  cored, seeded, and finely
  chopped
1 large firm, red plum tomato,
  skinned, seeded, and finely
  chopped
¼ teaspoon ground coriander
2 tablespoons finely chopped
  cilantro leaves
1 firm, ripe avocado, halved,
  pitted, peeled, and
  chopped
salt and freshly ground black
  pepper

1 To make the salsa, plunge the corn ears into a saucepan of boiling water, return to a boil, and blanch for 3–4 minutes. Drain, rub with a little of the olive oil, and place on an oiled barbecue grill over hot coals for 10–15 minutes, turning occasionally, until tender and well toasted. Allow to cool slightly, then scrape the kernels into a bowl and set aside to cool.

2 Add the onion to the corn with the lime juice, jalapeño sauce, chili, red pepper, tomato, ground coriander, cilantro, the remaining oil, and salt and pepper. Toss gently to combine, then fold in the avocado. Taste and adjust the seasoning as necessary. Cover and chill for at least 30 minutes for the flavors to develop.

3 Brush the tuna steaks with a little of the olive oil. Cook on an oiled barbecue grill over hot coals for 2 minutes on each side. Serve with the salsa.

serves **4**
preparation time **15 minutes, plus marinating**
cooking time **6–8 minutes**

Miso-grilled salmon kebabs
with cucumber salad

2 tablespoons soy sauce
2 tablespoons sake or dry
   sherry
2 tablespoons honey
2 tablespoons miso paste
4 skinless salmon fillets,
   about 7 oz each, cut into
   cubes
2 small cucumbers, seeded
   and sliced
1 red bird's eye chili, seeded
   and finely chopped
plain boiled rice, to serve

dressing
3 tablespoons rice wine
   vinegar
3 tablespoons superfine sugar
3 tablespoons water
½ teaspoon salt

1 Stir together the soy sauce, sake or sherry, honey, and miso paste until smooth then pour into a shallow dish. Add the salmon fillets, cover, and marinate in the refrigerator for 4 hours, or preferably overnight.

2 Meanwhile, combine the dressing ingredients in a small saucepan and heat gently to dissolve the sugar, then set aside to cool. Mix in the cucumbers and chili.

3 Thread the cubes of salmon onto 4 presoaked wooden skewers. Cook on an oiled barbecue grill over hot coals for 3–4 minutes on each side until the fish is browned and cooked through. Serve with the cucumber salad and some boiled rice.

BARBIE TIP
There are several different varieties of miso paste, each with its own distinct flavor. Choose red or brown miso for this dish, rather than the milder, sweeter white paste.

serves **4**
preparation time **10 minutes, plus marinating**
cooking time **15–20 minutes**

Grilled miso cod
with bok choy

**4 chunky cod fillets, about
 6 oz each
4 heads bok choy, halved
 lengthwise
olive oil**

miso sauce
**⅓ cup miso paste
4 tablespoons soy sauce
4 tablespoons sake
4 tablespoons rice wine
 (mirin)
4 tablespoons superfine sugar**

1 First make the miso sauce. Place the miso paste, soy sauce, sake, rice wine, and sugar in a small saucepan and heat gently until the sugar has dissolved. Simmer very gently for about 5 minutes, stirring frequently. Remove from the heat and set aside to cool.

2 Arrange the cod fillets in a snug-fitting dish and cover with the cold miso sauce. Rub the sauce over the fillets so that they are completely covered and allow to marinate for at least 6 hours, but preferably overnight.

3 Bring a saucepan of water to a boil, then plunge in the bok choy and blanch for 1–2 minutes, then drain. Brush a little oil over the cut side of the bok choy.

4 Remove the cod fillets from the miso sauce and place them on an oiled barbecue grill. Cook for 2–3 minutes over medium heat, then carefully turn them over and cook for an additional 2–3 minutes until they are cooked through. When you turn the cod over, add the bok choy, cut-side down, and cook for about 2 minutes until hot and lightly browned. Remove the cod and bok choy, arrange on a serving plate, and serve immediately.

serves **4**
preparation time **10 minutes, plus marinating**
cooking time **4–6 minutes**

Mediterranean shrimp
with spicy marinade

**1 lb raw jumbo shrimp, in
    their shells
4 tablespoons olive oil
2 garlic cloves, finely crushed
1 teaspoon ground cumin
½ teaspoon ground ginger
1 teaspoon paprika
¼ teaspoon cayenne pepper
handful of cilantro leaves,
    finely chopped
salt
lemon wedges, to serve**

1 Peel and devein most of the shrimp, leaving a few whole, since they look so attractive.

2 Mix the olive oil, garlic, cumin, ginger, paprika, cayenne pepper, and cilantro in a bowl. Add the shrimp and toss to combine. Season with salt and let marinate while you light the barbecue.

3 Divide the shrimp between four metal or presoaked wooden skewers. Place them on an oiled barbecue grill and cook them over medium coals for 2–3 minutes on each side until they are thoroughly cooked. Serve hot, accompanied by lemon wedges.

serves **2**
preparation time **20 minutes, plus time to prepare the lobster**
cooking time **10 minutes**

Garlicky lobster
with lemon butter and mayonnaise

1 steamed lobster, 2–3 lb
⅓ cup butter, at room
temperature
1 garlic clove, crushed
1 tablespoon capers in
sea salt, rinsed and drained
1 tablespoon lemon juice
1 tablespoon chopped chervil
1 tablespoon chopped
flat-leaf parsley
1 teaspoon chopped tarragon

mayonnaise
2 egg yolks, at room
temperature
pinch of salt
⅔ cup groundnut oil
1¼ cups mild extra virgin
olive oil
1 tablespoon lemon juice
1 teaspoon wholegrain
mustard
salt and freshly ground black
pepper

1 Using a very sharp knife, cut the lobster in half lengthwise and remove the intestinal vein that runs down the back. Crack the claws and set aside.

2 To make the mayonnaise, place the egg yolks in a bowl with a pinch of salt and beat (an electric mixer fitted with a beater attachment works best) for 1 minute until the eggs are frothy. Very slowly, add the groundnut oil drop by drop until you have a thick glossy mixture. Now do the same with the olive oil, beating continuously until all the oil has been incorporated. Still beating, drizzle in the lemon juice and the mustard. Season with salt and pepper to taste.

3 Mix 2 tablespoons of the butter with the garlic and smear the lobster flesh with the garlicky butter. Lay the shell side of the lobster on an oiled barbecue grill and cook over medium coals for 3–4 minutes, then turn it onto the cut side and cook for about 2 minutes until the flesh and claws are hot and browned. Remove from the barbecue and keep warm while you prepare the lemon butter.

4 Melt the remaining butter in a small pan and heat until it begins to turn golden and smells nutty. Stir in the capers, lemon juice, and herbs, then remove from the heat.

5 Serve the lobster halves with the lemon caper butter and a small dish of the homemade mayonnaise.

BARBIE TIP
You can buy ready-cooked lobsters from a fish merchant or some supermarkets, but langoustines and jumbo shrimp also work very well.

From divine vegetable
accompaniments to
irresistible meals for
the vegetarian, this
chapter is packed
with inspired ideas
for meat-free dishes.
Choose a selection
of dishes to create a
feast that will appeal
to vegetarians and
meat-eaters alike.

Vegetables and Vegetarian

serves **4**
preparation time **25 minutes**
cooking time **30 minutes**

Vegetable kebabs
with spicy peanut sauce

2 tablespoons lime juice
1 tablespoon blackstrap
  molasses
1 tablespoon soy sauce
1 tablespoon sweet
  chili sauce
1 tablespoon olive oil
4 oz tofu, cubed
1 cooking apple, quartered
4 pineapple chunks
4 mango chunks
4 tomatoes, halved
  horizontally
1 red onion, quartered
8 mushrooms, halved
1 red bell pepper, cored,
  seeded, and quartered
1 green bell pepper, cored,
  seeded, and quartered
1 corn ear, cooked and sliced
  into 8 rounds
1 sweet potato, boiled and
  thickly sliced
1 zucchini, thickly sliced
1 cup spicy peanut sauce
  (see page 15)
boiled brown basmati rice
  or stir-fried rice noodles,
  to serve

to garnish
lime wedges
sprinkling of grated coconut
  and chopped cilantro leaves

1 Pour the lime juice, molasses, soy sauce, sweet chili sauce, and oil into a large bowl and mix well. Add the tofu and all the prepared fruit and vegetables, and stir until thoroughly coated.

2 Thread chunks of fruit and vegetables onto 8 presoaked wooden skewers, alternating ingredients to give a range of color and texture. Place on an oiled barbecue grill and cook over medium coals for 8–10 minutes until browned on all sides.

3 Serve the kebabs on a bed of brown basmati rice or stir-fried rice noodles with the peanut sauce poured over the top. Garnish each serving with a wedge of lime and a sprinkling of grated coconut and chopped cilantro.

serves **4**
preparation time **10–15 minutes, plus chilling**
cooking time **20–25 minutes**

Potato wedges
with hot tomato salsa

4 large potatoes
4 tablespoons olive oil
salad leaves, to serve

hot tomato salsa
1 small red onion, finely
chopped
1 garlic clove, finely chopped
1 lb sweet ripe tomatoes,
skinned, seeded, and
chopped
1–2 moderately hot red
chilies, seeded and finely
chopped
3 tablespoons finely chopped
cilantro leaves
1 tablespoon finely chopped
parsley
1 tablespoon lime juice
3 tablespoons extra virgin
olive oil
pinch of sugar
salt and freshly ground black
pepper
salad leaves, to serve

1 To prepare the tomato salsa, place the onion, garlic, tomatoes, and chilies in a bowl. Add the cilantro and parsley and stir in the lime juice and olive oil. Season with a pinch of sugar and salt and pepper and mix lightly.

2 Cover and chill for 30–60 minutes, to give the flavors time to develop.

3 Place the whole, unpeeled potatoes in a large pan of cold water, bring to a boil, reduce the heat, and simmer for 15–20 minutes or until just tender. Drain, and when cool enough to handle, cut each potato into large wedges.

4 Brush the potatoes wedges with the oil and lay on an oiled barbecue grill. Cook over hot coals for 5–6 minutes, turning frequently, until golden brown. Serve with the tomato salsa and some salad leaves.

serves **4**
preparation time **15 minutes**
cooking time **10 minutes**

Nut koftas
with minted yogurt

5–6 tablespoons vegetable oil
1 onion, chopped
½ teaspoon crushed red pepper
2 garlic cloves, roughly chopped
1 tablespoon medium curry paste
14 oz can cannellini beans, rinsed and drained
1½ cups ground almonds
½ cup chopped honey-roasted or salted almonds
1 egg
¾ cup plain yogurt
2 tablespoons chopped mint
1 tablespoon lemon juice
salt and freshly ground black pepper
warm naan bread, to serve
salad leaves, to garnish

1 Heat 3 tablespoons of the oil in a skillet, add the onion and fry for 4 minutes. Add the crushed pepper, garlic, and curry paste and fry for a minute more.

2 Transfer to a food processor or blender with the beans, ground almonds, chopped almonds, egg, and a little salt and pepper, and process until the mixture starts to bind together.

3 With lightly floured hands, take about one-eighth of the mixture and mold it around a presoaked wooden skewer, forming it into a sausage about 1 inch thick. Make 7 more koftas in the same way. Place the skewers on an oiled barbecue grill over medium coals and brush with another tablespoon of the oil. Cook for about 5 minutes, until golden, turning once.

4 Meanwhile, mix together the yogurt and mint in a small serving bowl and season to taste with salt and pepper. In a separate bowl, mix together the remaining oil, lemon juice, and a little salt and pepper.

5 Brush the koftas with the lemon dressing and serve with the yogurt dressing on warm naan bread garnished with salad leaves.

BARBIE TIP
Be sure to oil the barbecue rack well before you place the koftas on it. They are a little crumbly and may be difficult to turn if they stick.

serves 4
preparation time **10 minutes**
cooking time **10 minutes**

Bean and pepper cakes
with lemon mayonnaise

3 oz green beans, roughly
chopped
2 tablespoons groundnut or
vegetable oil, plus extra
for frying
1 red bell pepper, cored,
seeded, and diced
4 garlic cloves, crushed
2 teaspoons mild chili powder
14 oz can red kidney beans,
rinsed and drained
1½ cups fresh white bread
crumbs
1 egg yolk
salt and freshly ground black
pepper

lemon mayonnaise
4 tablespoons mayonnaise
finely grated zest of 1 lemon
1 teaspoon lemon juice

1 Blanch the green beans in a pan of lightly salted boiling water for 1–2 minutes, or until softened. Drain. Meanwhile, heat the groundnut or vegetable oil in a skillet and add the red pepper, garlic, and chili powder. Cook for 2 minutes.

2 Transfer the mixture to a blender or food processor and add the red kidney beans, bread crumbs, and egg yolk. Process very briefly until the ingredients are roughly chopped. Add the drained green beans and season to taste with salt and pepper. Process until the ingredients are just combined.

3 Turn the mixture into a bowl and divide it into 8 portions. Using lightly floured hands, shape the portions into little cakes. Mix the mayonnaise with the lemon zest and juice and season to taste with salt and pepper. Set aside.

4 Heat the oil for frying in a large skillet and cook the cakes for about 3 minutes on each side until crisp and golden. Serve with the lemon mayonnaise.

BARBIE TIP
These crisp bean cakes, packed into warm pita breads and served with a salad, make a fairly substantial lunch or supper dish. Any unbaked cakes, interleaved with waxed paper, will keep in the refrigerator for a day or so.

serves **4**
preparation time **15 minutes**
cooking time **5–6 minutes**

Barbecued asparagus
with balsamic tomato dressing

**2 tablespoons balsamic
vinegar
1–2 garlic cloves, crushed
12 oz tomatoes, skinned,
seeded, and chopped
7 tablespoons extra virgin
olive oil
1 lb young asparagus spears
⅓ cup pine nuts, toasted
1 oz Parmesan cheese,
shaved into thin slivers
sea salt flakes and freshly
ground black pepper
warm bread, to serve**

1 Place the vinegar, garlic, chopped tomatoes, and 5 tablespoons of the olive oil in a small bowl. Mix well to combine and set aside.

2 Trim the asparagus spears to remove any tough, fibrous stems. Brush the asparagus with the remaining olive oil and cook on an oiled barbecue grill over medium coals for 5–6 minutes until tender.

3 Divide the asparagus between 4 warmed serving plates. Spoon over the balsamic vinegar and tomato dressing, top with the pine nuts and Parmesan slivers, and sprinkle with the sea salt flakes and pepper. Serve at once with plenty of warm bread to mop up the juices.

BARBIE TIP
Plainly grilled, asparagus is delicious served with fish, poultry, or meat.

serves **4**
preparation time **10 minutes, plus setting**
cooking time **10–15 minutes**

Parmesan and herb polenta wedges
with tomato and mint salsa

2½ cups water
1 cup quick-cooking polenta
⅓ cup butter
1 cup freshly grated Parmesan
  cheese
2 tablespoons chopped chives
2 tablespoons roughly
  chopped parsley
2 tablespoons chopped
  chervil
salt and freshly ground black
  pepper

spicy cherry tomato salsa
10 oz ripe cherry tomatoes,
  quartered
2 small red chilies, seeded
  and finely chopped
1 small red onion, finely
  chopped
2 tablespoons chili oil
2 tablespoons extra virgin
  olive oil
2 tablespoons lime juice
2 tablespoons shredded mint

1 Bring the measured water to a simmer in a saucepan, pour in the polenta and beat well with a wooden spoon until it is thick and smooth. Reduce the heat and continue stirring for about 5 minutes (or according to the package instructions) to cook the polenta.

2 Remove the pan from the heat and add the butter, Parmesan, chives, parsley, and chervil and stir until well combined. Season with salt and pepper then turn into a greased 10 inch cake pan, at least 1 inch deep. Smooth the top with the back of a spoon and allow to set for about 5–10 minutes.

3 Combine all the salsa ingredients in a bowl and season with salt and pepper to taste. Set aside.

4 Carefully remove the set polenta from the cake pan, transfer it to a cutting board, and cut it into 8 wedges.

5 Place the polenta wedges in a barbecue pan, and place this on a barbecue grill. Cook over medium coals for 2–3 minutes on each side, until heated through and golden. Serve 2 wedges per person with a spoonful of the salsa on the side.

serves **4**
preparation time **10 minutes, plus marinating**
cooking time **about 8 minutes**

Grilled thyme-marinated goat cheeses
with walnut bread

4 crottins de chèvre, or small, firm goat cheeses, halved vertically
4 slices walnut bread

marinade
¾ cup olive oil, plus extra if necessary
3 tablespoons walnut oil
1 teaspoon dried thyme or lemon thyme sprigs
grated zest of 1 lemon
1 teaspoon crushed red pepper
1 small garlic clove, thinly sliced
8 black peppercorns
8 large vine leaves in brine, rinsed well in cold water

to serve
green salad
balsamic vinegar

1 Place all the marinade ingredients in a 2 cup screw-top jar and mix well. Add the halved goat cheeses and allow to marinate in a cool place for at least 24 hours and up to 3 days.

2 Remove the cheeses from the marinade and drain on paper towels to remove any excess oil. Place the vine leaves on a cutting board and place half a goat cheese in the center of each one. Wrap the leaves around the cheese so that it is sealed inside.

3 Place the walnut bread on an oiled barbecue grill and cook over medium coals for 2 minutes. Keep the bread warm. Place the 8 leaf parcels (seam side down) and the tomato halves on the barbecue grill and cook for 8 minutes, turning once, until the leaves are crispy and the cheese is melting and the tomatoes are soft.

4 Serve the goat cheeses immediately with the grilled walnut bread and a little green salad, drizzled with the marinating oil and some balsamic vinegar.

serves **4**
preparation time **15 minutes**
cooking time **30–40 minutes**

Corn ears
with skorthalia

4 whole corn ears, with husks

skorthalia
**1 cup fresh white bread
crumbs**
¾ cup ground almonds
4 garlic cloves, crushed
2 tablespoons lemon juice
⅔ cup olive oil
**salt and freshly ground black
pepper**

1 To make the skorthalia, place the bread crumbs in a bowl and cover with water. Soak for 5 minutes, then squeeze out the excess liquid and place the crumbs in a blender or food processor. Add the ground almonds, garlic, and 1 tablespoon of the lemon juice, and process until well mixed. With the motor running, gradually add the olive oil in a thin, steady stream until the mixture resembles mayonnaise. Add more lemon juice and salt and pepper to taste.

2 Pull down the husks of the corn ears and remove the inner skins. Pull the husks back over the corn ears. Place on an oiled barbecue grill over hot coals and cook for 30–40 minutes, until the kernels are juicy and come away easily from the core.

3 To serve, pull back the husks of the corn ears and spread with the skorthalia.

BARBIE TIP
Skorthalia is a garlic sauce that can also be served with other vegetables, or grilled meat or fish. It goes particularly well with barbecued zucchini and fennel wedges.

Salads

No barbecue is complete without a selection of fabulous salads. Try tangy Watermelon and Feta Salad with robust meaty grills, or wholesome Roasted Vegetable and Bean Salad with spicy skewers and chargrilled chicken.

serves **4**
preparation time **15 minutes, plus resting**
cooking time **10 minutes**

Warm tea-smoked salmon salad
with wilted arugula

4 salmon fillets, about 4 oz each
8 cherry tomatoes, halved
2½ cups arugula

smoke mix
8 tablespoons Jasmine tea
leaves
8 tablespoons brown sugar
8 tablespoons long-grain rice

dressing
1 shallot, finely chopped
1 garlic clove, finely chopped
few thyme leaves
1 teaspoon Dijon mustard
2 teaspoons white wine
vinegar
4–5 tablespoons extra virgin
olive oil
salt and freshly ground black
pepper

1 Mix together all the ingredients for the smoke mix. Line a wok with a large sheet of foil, allowing it to overhang the edges, and pour in the smoke mix. Place a trivet over the top. Cover with a tight-fitting lid and heat for 5 minutes or until the mixture is smoking.

2 Meanwhile, remove any bones from the salmon with tweezers. Place the tomatoes in a bowl with the arugula.

3 Quickly remove the lid from the wok and place the salmon fillets, skin-side down, on the trivet. Cover and cook over a high heat for 5 minutes. Remove from the heat and set aside, covered, for another 3 minutes.

4 Meanwhile, make the dressing. Place the shallot, garlic, thyme leaves, mustard, vinegar, and oil in a bowl, and season to taste with salt and pepper. Beat thoroughly to combine.

5 Flake the salmon into the salad, add the dressing, and toss well. Serve immediately.

BARBIE TIP
Smoking fish and meat over a mixture of tea leaves, sugar, and rice is a method widely used in Chinese cooking, but this dish adapts the method for Western tastes.

serves **4**
preparation time **10–15 minutes**
cooking time **5–6 minutes**

Smoked chicken and avocado salad
with tarragon and mustard dressing

6 tablespoons olive oil
4 slices of day-old bread,
cut into ½ inch dice
1 lb smoked chicken breast
slices
3 small crisp lettuces or
lettuce hearts
1 large ripe avocado, peeled,
pitted, and diced
¼ cup freshly grated
Parmesan cheese

dressing
½ cup extra virgin olive oil
2 tablespoons tarragon
vinegar
1 tablespoon wholegrain
mustard
1 tablespoon chopped
tarragon
1 teaspoon superfine sugar
salt and freshly ground black
pepper

1 To make the croutons, heat the oil in a skillet and fry the bread cubes, stirring constantly, for 5–6 minutes until golden on all sides. Drain on paper towels.

2 Cut the chicken breast slices into bite-size pieces and place in a large bowl. Add the lettuce leaves to the chicken with the avocado, croutons, and Parmesan.

3 Beat the dressing ingredients together and season with salt and pepper. Pour the dressing over the salad and toss well until the salad is evenly coated. Serve at once.

BARBIE TIP
Because smoked chicken is hot-smoked, it is already cooked and ready to eat. You can take advantage of such tasty cooked ingredients to throw together salads in minutes.

serves **4**
preparation time **15 minutes**

Orange and avocado salad
with spicy citrus dressing

4 large juicy oranges
2 small ripe avocados, peeled
 and pitted
2 teaspoons cardamom pods
3 tablespoons extra virgin
 olive oil
1 tablespoon honey
pinch of ground allspice
2 teaspoons lemon juice
salt and freshly ground black
 pepper
watercress sprigs, to garnish

1 Cut the skin and the white membrane off the oranges. Working over a bowl to catch the juice, cut between the membranes to remove the segments; reserve the juice. Slice the avocados and toss gently with the orange segments. Pile onto serving plates.

2 Reserve a few whole cardamom pods for garnishing. Crush the remainder to extract the seeds, using a pestle and mortar or a small bowl and the end of a rolling pin. Pick out and discard the pods.

3 Mix the seeds with the oil, honey, allspice, lemon juice, salt and pepper to taste, and the reserved orange juice. Garnish the salad with the watercress sprigs and reserved cardamom pods and serve with the dressing spooned over the top.

serves **4**
preparation time **10 minutes**

Fig, mozzarella, and prosciutto salad
with verjuice dressing

8–12 ripe black figs
8 oz buffalo mozzarella
8 prosciutto slices
a few basil leaves

dressing
3 tablespoons extra virgin
**   olive oil**
1 tablespoon verjuice
salt and freshly ground black
**   pepper**

1 Cut the figs into quarters, tear the mozzarella and prosciutto into bite-size pieces, and arrange on a large platter with the basil leaves.

2 Beat together the extra virgin olive oil, verjuice, and salt and pepper to taste. Drizzle the dressing over the salad and serve at once.

BARBIE TIP
Verjuice, made from unripe grapes, has a strong, acidic flavor and is used in cooking as an alternative to lemon juice or vinegar. It gives the dressing a lovely flavor. If you cannot find it, use a good-quality white wine vinegar sweetened with a pinch of sugar instead.

serves **4**
preparation time **10 minutes**
cooking time **2 minutes**

Watermelon and feta salad
with fruity dressing

1 tablespoon black sesame
  seeds
1 lb watermelon, peeled,
  seeded, and diced
6 oz feta cheese, diced
1¼ cups arugula leaves
handful of mint, parsley,
  and cilantro sprigs
6 tablespoons extra virgin
  olive oil
1 tablespoon orange flower
  water
1½ tablespoons lemon juice
1 teaspoon pomegranate
  syrup (optional)
½ teaspoon sugar
salt and freshly ground black
  pepper
toasted pita breads, to serve
  (optional)

1 Dry-fry the sesame seeds for a few minutes until aromatic, then set aside. Arrange the watermelon and feta on a large plate with the arugula and herbs.

2 Beat together the oil, orange flower water, lemon juice, pomegranate syrup, if using, and sugar, then season to taste with salt and pepper. Drizzle the dressing over the salad, sprinkle with the sesame seeds, and serve with toasted pita breads, if desired.

serves **4**
preparation time **15 minutes**
cooking time **up to 40 minutes**

Roasted vegetable and bean salad
with herb vinaigrette

1 eggplant
1 red bell pepper, halved, cored, and seeded
1 yellow bell pepper, halved, cored, and seeded
1 zucchini
4 garlic cloves
4 tablespoons olive oil
1 teaspoon coarse sea salt
1¾ cups cooked flageolet beans
2 tablespoons chopped mixed herbs (parsley, oregano or cilantro, and mint)
6 tablespoons Classic vinaigrette (see page 14)
pepper
mint leaves, to garnish

1 Cut all the vegetables into strips and put them into a roasting pan. Add the garlic cloves. Sprinkle with the olive oil, salt, and some pepper.

2 Place the pan in a preheated oven, 425°F, and roast for up to 40 minutes, or until the vegetables are cooked. Transfer the vegetables to a shallow bowl and allow to cool.

3 Add the beans and toss lightly. Stir the herbs into the vinaigrette, pour it over the salad, and serve garnished with the mint leaves.

BARBIE TIP
Other vegetables, including fennel, tomatoes, baby squash, and mild chilies, would also work well in this salad.

serves **4**
preparation time **10 minutes, plus cooling**
cooking time **15 minutes**

Bulgar wheat salad
with fennel, orange, and spinach

¾ **cup bulgar wheat**
1 tablespoon olive oil
2 fennel bulbs, finely sliced
3½ **cups baby spinach leaves**
3 oranges, segmented
2 tablespoons pumpkin
seeds, toasted

dressing
4 tablespoons plain yogurt
2 tablespoons chopped
cilantro leaves
½ **small cucumber, finely**
chopped
1 tablespoon extra virgin
olive oil
salt and freshly ground black
pepper

1 Prepare the bulgar wheat according to the package instructions. Set aside to cool. Heat the oil in a skillet, add the fennel, and fry for 8–10 minutes until tender and browned. Add the spinach to the pan and stir through until it is just wilted.

2 Toss the fennel and spinach mixture with the bulgar wheat, then add the orange segments and pumpkin seeds.

3 Mix all the dressing ingredients together, stir through the salad, and serve.

makes **1½ cups**
preparation time **10 minutes, plus chilling**

Onion and tomato salsa
with cilantro

1 red onion, finely chopped
14 oz small vine-ripened tomatoes, halved, seeded, and chopped
2 garlic cloves, crushed
¾ cup chopped cilantro leaves
salt and freshly ground black pepper

1 Place the red onion, tomatoes, garlic, and cilantro leaves in a bowl and mix together. Season lightly with salt and pepper, then cover and chill for at least 30 minutes for the flavors to develop.

BARBIE TIP
Serve with cold meats or as a side dish with curries and other spicy foods.

serves **2**
preparation time **10 minutes**
cooking time **10–12 minutes**

Mixed bean and chorizo salad
with lemon dressing

¾ cup fresh or frozen green
   beans
1¼ cups frozen baby fava
   beans
4 oz chorizo sausage, diced
½ small red onion, finely
   chopped
3 tablespoons chopped
   parsley
salt and freshly ground black
   pepper
whole-wheat bread, to serve

dressing
2 tablespoons extra virgin
   olive oil
juice of half lemon
1 garlic clove, crushed
   (optional)

1 Plunge the green and fava beans into a saucepan of boiling water and cook for 3 minutes, or until tender. Drain, rinse under cold running water, drain again, then cut the green beans into 3 pieces.

2 Place the chorizo in a skillet and cook over a high heat for 6–8 minutes, turning occasionally, until browned and piping hot. Set aside.

3 To make the dressing, mix together the oil, lemon juice, and garlic, if using, in a salad bowl. Season to taste with salt and pepper and add the green and fava beans, the chorizo, onion, and parsley, then toss together. Serve with warmed whole-wheat bread.

BARBIE TIP
Quick and easy to prepare, this salad makes a great supper dish and any leftovers can be stored in a small container in the refrigerator and used next day.

Desserts

Whether it's a Classic Lemon Tart that you've made in advance, or some Barbecued Honeyed Peaches to cook over the fading embers of the barbecue, this chapter is packed with mouth-watering desserts to make an impressive end to the perfect barbecue.

serves **4**
preparation time **15–20 minutes, plus chilling**

Summer fruit skewers
with banana yogurt

4 thin lemon grass stalks
2⅔ cups strawberries, rinsed and halved
3 nectarines or peaches, rinsed, halved, pitted, and thickly sliced
4 kiwifruit, peeled and thickly sliced
grated zest and juice of 1 lime
1 banana
¾ cup virtually fat-free plain yogurt

1 Cut the lemon grass stalks in half lengthwise and peel off the outer grubby leaves. Using the clean stalks as skewers, thread strawberries, nectarines, and kiwifruit alternately on to the lemon grass until all the stalks have been filled. Place them on a plate and drizzle the lime juice over the fruit. Chill until needed.

2 Just before serving, mash the banana with a fork, then stir it into the yogurt with the lime zest. Spoon the sauce into a small bowl and serve with the fruit skewers.

BARBIE TIP
Since banana discolors with standing, the sauce is best made just before serving or no more than 30 minutes in advance.

serves **4**
preparation time **5 minutes**
cooking time **10 minutes**

Barbecued figs
with yogurt and honey

8 ripe figs
4 tablespoons plain yogurt
2 tablespoons honey

1 Wrap each fig in a parcel of double-thickness foil and place on a barbecue grill. Cook over medium coals for 8 minutes, turning occasionally, until the figs are hot and slightly soft. Remove them, unwrap them, and cut in half.

2 Arrange the figs on 4 plates and serve with a spoonful of plain yogurt and some honey spooned over the top.

serves **4**
preparation time **5 minutes**
cooking time **10–12 minutes**

Blackened bananas
with mascarpone and rum cream

1–2 tablespoons superfine
  sugar
½ teaspoon ground cinnamon
2 teaspoons rum
1 cup mascarpone cheese
8 small bananas

1 Mix the sugar, cinnamon, and rum in a bowl. Stir in the mascarpone, mix well, and set aside.

2 Place the whole, unpeeled bananas on a barbecue grill over hot coals and cook for 10–12 minutes, turning the bananas as the skins darken, until they are black all over and the flesh is very tender.

3 To serve, split the bananas open and spread the flesh with the mascarpone cream.

BARBIE TIP
If you don't have any mascarpone cheese, simply serve the bananas with some whipped cream.

serves **6**
preparation time **15 minutes, plus freezing**

Strawberry ice cream
with wild strawberries

3 cups strawberries, hulled
4 tablespoons fresh orange
   juice
¾ cup superfine sugar
2 cups whipping cream

to decorate (optional)
wild strawberries
strawberry syrup

1 Finely mash the strawberries and mix with the orange juice to form a smooth puree. Stir in the sugar.

2 Whip the cream until it forms soft peaks and fold it into the puree. Pour the mixture into a 2 lb loaf pan. Freeze for 1½ hours or until partly frozen.

3 Turn the mixture into a bowl, break it up with a fork and then beat until smooth. Return the mixture to the loaf pan and freeze for at least 5 hours until completely frozen.

4 Transfer the ice cream to the refrigerator 30 minutes before serving, to soften. Decorate with wild strawberries and strawberry syrup, if desired.

BARBIE TIP
If using an ice cream maker, follow the recipe until the end of step 1. Place the mixture in the machine and add the cream. Churn and freeze following the manufacturer's instructions.

serves **2**
preparation time **5 minutes, plus chilling**
cooking time **5 minutes**

Summer fruit compote
with yogurt

**1½ cups mixed summer fruit
(raspberries, blueberries,
and strawberries), thawed
if frozen
finely grated zest and juice of
1 large orange
1 tablespoon red currant jelly
1 cup Greek or whole milk
yogurt, to serve**

1 Place the fruit, orange zest and juice, and red currant jelly in a large saucepan. Cover and cook gently for 5 minutes, or until the juices flow and the fruit is softened. Remove from the heat and set aside.

2 Chill the fruit compote for at least 1 hour. Serve with spoonfuls of Greek or whole milk yogurt.

serves **4**
preparation time **10 minutes**
cooking time **14 minutes**

Panettone and peaches
with sweet mascarpone

**4 slices of panettone (Italian
yeast cake)**
4 peaches, halved and pitted
½ cup ground almonds
2 tablespoons brown sugar
¾ cup mascarpone cheese
honey, for drizzling

1 Toast the panettone slices on an oiled barbecue grill over medium coals for 4 minutes on each side. Remove and keep warm.

2 Cut the peach halves into wedges and cook them on the barbecue grill for 3 minutes on each side. Meanwhile, mix the ground almonds with the sugar and mascarpone to get a marbled effect.

3 Divide the peach wedges between the toasted panettone slices. To serve, add a generous spoonful of the mascarpone mixture and drizzle honey over the peaches.

BARBIE TIP
Although a traditional Italian Christmas treat, panettone is available throughout the year, but if you can't find it, try brioche bread as an alternative.

serves **4**
preparation time **15 minutes**
cooking time **12–15 minutes**

Barbecued honeyed peaches
with amaretti

4 ripe peaches
1¼ cups Marsala
4 tablespoons honey
1 strip of orange rind
2 tablespoons butter, melted
4 amaretti cookies
vanilla ice cream, to serve

1 Cut a small cross in the top and bottom of each peach and place them in a pan of boiling water, leave for 20 seconds, then transfer with a slotted spoon to a bowl of cold water. Peel the peaches, cut them in half lengthwise, and remove the pits.

2 Place the Marsala, honey, and orange rind in a large saucepan, bring to a boil, then simmer for 2 minutes. Add the peach halves and simmer for 3–4 minutes until they are just tender. Remove the pan from the heat and allow the peaches to cool in the syrup.

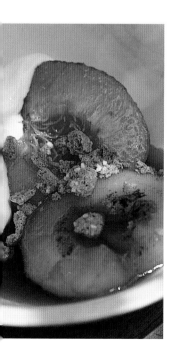

3 Remove the peaches with a slotted spoon and place the remaining syrup in a small saucepan. Bring to a boil and reduce by half.

4 Brush the peaches with the melted butter and place them on an oiled barbecue grill over medium coals for 5–7 minutes, turning once.

5 Transfer the hot peaches to serving plates, spoon over a little of the reduced syrup and crumble over the amaretti cookies. Serve with vanilla ice cream.

BARBIE TIP
Use very ripe peaches because they have the best flavor, but be careful when turning them, since they will be soft.

serves **4**
preparation time **10 minutes, plus infusing and standing**
cooking time **about 1 hour**

Baked lemon custards
with bay leaves

12 fresh bay leaves, bruised
2 tablespoons finely grated
lemon zest
⅔ cup heavy cream
4 eggs, plus 1 egg yolk
⅔ cup superfine sugar
6 tablespoons lemon juice
bay leaves, to decorate

1 Place the bay leaves, lemon zest, and cream in a small saucepan and heat gently until it reaches boiling point. Remove from the heat and set aside for 2 hours to infuse.

2 Beat together the eggs, egg yolk, and sugar until the mixture is pale and creamy, then beat in the lemon juice. Strain the cream mixture through a fine strainer into the egg mixture and stir until combined.

3 Pour the custard into 4 individual ramekins and place on a baking sheet. Bake in a preheated oven, 250°F, for 50 minutes, or until the custards are almost set in the middle. Allow to stand until cold and then chill until required. Let the custards return to room temperature before serving. Decorate with bay leaves.

serves **8**
preparation time **20 minutes, plus chilling**
cooking time **40–45 minutes**

Uncooked lime cheesecake
with strawberries and blueberries

¼ **cup butter**
2 tablespoons corn syrup
2 cups crushed malted milk
cookies

filling
1 cup mascarpone cheese
¾ **cup virtually fat-free plain**
yogurt
¼ **cup superfine sugar, sifted**
grated zest and juice of
2 limes
⅔ **cup heavy cream**

to decorate
1½ **cups strawberries, halved**
or sliced, if large
1 cup fresh blueberries
confectioners' sugar, sifted
(optional)

1 To make the base, melt the butter and syrup in a saucepan. Place the cookies in a plastic bag, crush finely with a rolling pin, then stir into the butter mixture. Mix well and press into the base of a 7 inch removable-bottomed, fluted tart pan.

2 Beat the mascarpone cheese in a bowl to soften it, then stir in the yogurt, sugar, and lime zest. Gradually beat in the lime juice.

3 In a second, smaller bowl, whip the cream until it forms soft peaks, then fold it into the mascarpone mixture. Spoon the creamy filling onto the cookie base and swirl the top with the back of a spoon.

4 Chill the cheesecake in the refrigerator for 3 hours or longer, if preferred. To serve, carefully remove the cheesecake from the pan and decorate with berries and a dusting of confectioners' sugar, if desired.

serves **4**
preparation time **25 minutes, plus freezing**
cooking time **4–5 minutes**

Lime and mango granita

¼ cup superfine sugar
1¼ cups water
finely grated zest and juice
   of 2 limes
1 large ripe mango
sliced mango, to decorate
   (optional)

1 Place the sugar, water, and lime zest in a small saucepan and heat gently for 4–5 minutes until the sugar has completely dissolved. Allow to cool.

2 Cut a thick slice off either side of the mango to reveal the large flat pit, then make criss-cross cuts in these slices and scoop the flesh away from the skin, using a spoon. Cut away the flesh surrounding the pit and remove the skin. Process the mango flesh in a blender or food processor until smooth.

3 Mix together the mango puree, sugar syrup, and lime juice, then pour it into a shallow metal dish so that it is about ¾ inch deep. Freeze for 1 hour.

4 Take the dish out of the freezer and mash the mixture with a fork to break up any large ice crystals. Return to the freezer and freeze for 1½ hours, beating the mixture with a fork at 30 minute intervals until the granita has the consistency of crushed ice.

5 Spoon the granita into 4 dishes and decorate with extra slices of mango, if desired. Transfer any remaining granita to a plastic container with a lid and return to the freezer.

BARBIE TIP
A can of mango in fruit juice makes a good alternative to fresh mango. Purée the fruit with the juice and add to the sugar syrup and lime juice.

serves **8**
preparation time **15 minutes**
cooking time **25–30 minutes**

Black Forest chocolate cake
with chocolate sauce

1⅔ cups self-rising whole-
  wheat flour
1 cup brown sugar
2 tablespoons cocoa powder
2 heaping teaspoons carob
  powder
½ cup sunflower oil
⅔ cup milk
1 tablespoon plain yogurt
  or coconut cream
2 teaspoons cider vinegar
pinch of salt
1 oz bittersweet chocolate
  (70 per cent cocoa solids)
fresh cherries or berries,
  to decorate
hot chocolate sauce, to serve

filling
4 tablespoons cream cheese
1 teaspoon lime zest
4 tablespoons morello cherry
  or blackberry jelly

sauce
7 oz dark chocolate, broken
  into pieces
4 tablespoons milk
3 tablespoons corn syrup
½ teaspoon vanilla extract
2 tablespoons unsalted butter

1 Oil two 8 inch circular layer cake pans and line them with nonstick parchment paper.

2 Place all the cake ingredients, except the chocolate, in a food processor and beat together thoroughly.

3 Coarsely grate or chop the chocolate and add to the cake mixture. Divide the mixture between the cake pans and level the tops with a spatula.

4 Bake the cakes in a preheated oven, 350°F, for 25–30 minutes, or until a toothpick inserted into the center of each cake comes out clean. Allow to cool a little, then turn out onto a cooling rack and leave until completely cold.

5 To make the sauce, put the chocolate, milk, corn syrup, and vanilla extract into a small, heavy saucepan and heat gently, stirring frequently, until the chocolate has melted. Stir in the butter. Continue stirring until the sauce is smooth, then pour it into a pitcher.

6 Place the cream cheese in a bowl and stir in the lime zest. Spread one side of a cold cake with the lime cream cheese, and spread the other cake with jelly. Sandwich them together and place on a serving plate.

7 Pour over the thick chocolate sauce and decorate the cake with fresh cherries or berries.

serves **8**
preparation time **20 minutes, plus chilling**
cooking time **40–45 minutes**

Classic lemon tart

1¾ cups all-purpose flour
½ teaspoon salt
½ cup chilled butter, diced
2 tablespoons confectioners'
sugar, plus extra for dusting
2 egg yolks
1–2 teaspoons cold water

filling
3 eggs, plus 1 egg yolk
2 cups heavy cream
½ cup superfine sugar
⅔ cup lemon juice

1 Place the flour in a bowl, add the salt and diced butter, and blend with the fingertips until the mixture resembles fine bread crumbs. Stir in the sugar and gradually work in the egg yolks and measured water to make a firm dough.

2 Knead the dough briefly on a lightly floured surface, then cover with plastic wrap and chill for 30 minutes. Roll out the dough and use it to line a 10 inch fluted tart pan. Prick the pastry shell with a fork and chill for 20 minutes.

3 Line the pastry shell with nonstick parchment paper, fill with pie weights and cook in a preheated oven, 400°F, for 10 minutes. Remove the paper and weights, and bake for 10 minutes more until crisp and golden. Remove from the oven and reduce the temperature to 300°F.

4 Beat together all the filling ingredients, pour them into the pie shell and bake for 20–25 minutes, or until the filling is just set. Allow the tart to cool completely, dust with confectioners' sugar, and serve.

Index

Acknowledgments

PHOTOGRAPHIC ACKNOWLEDGMENTS

Getty Images 16–17; /Sara Gray 106–107; /David Loftus 74–75; /Brian Stablyk 36–37; /Jonelle Weaver 88–89. **Octopus Publishing Group Limited**/Frank Adam 12; /Clive Bozzard-Hill 123 ; /Jean Cazals 28; /Stephen Conroy 112; /Gus Filgate 4, 44, 77, 103; /Jeremy Hopley 3, 5, 9, 49, 53, 65, 79, 81; /David Jordan 2, 6, 27, 47, 51, 91, 105; /William Lingwood 24, 29, 39, 59, 66, 69, 92, 97, 115, 121; /James Merrell 1, 19, 33, 41, 54–55, 86, 111, 117; /Hilary Moore 11; /Alan Newman 31; /Lis Parsons 95, 99, 118, 125; /William Reavell 100; /Gareth Sambidge 20, 30, 35, 38, 43, 50, 57, 60, 63, 70, 73, 83, 85, 102, 109; /Ian Wallace 15, 23.

Executive Editor Nicky Hill
Project Editor Jessica Cowie
Executive Art Editor Tokiko Morishima
Designer Lisa Tai
Picture Researcher Sophie Delpech
Production Controller Nigel Reed